5-16-60   56-5188

ALBERT SCHWEITZER: MAN OF MERCY

BOOKS BY JACQUELYN BERRILL

WONDERS OF THE SEASHORE

WONDERS OF THE WOODLAND ANIMALS

STRANGE NURSERIES, A WONDER BOOK

WONDERS OF THE WILD, ANIMAL PORTRAITS AND
PRIVATE LIVES

ALBERT SCHWEITZER: MAN OF MERCY

by JACQUELYN BERRILL

Albert Schweitzer:
Man of Mercy

ILLUSTRATED WITH DRAWINGS BY THE AUTHOR
AND WITH PHOTOGRAPHS

DODD, MEAD & COMPANY · New York

Fourth Printing

Library of Congress Catalog Card Number: 56-5188

Printed in the United States of America
by The Cornwall Press, Inc., Cornwall, N. Y.

To MY THREE CHILDREN
Michael
Elsilyn
Peggy

hoping that they will see in
this simple story of a man
a model of high endeavor

Acknowledgments

I am indebted first and foremost to Albert Schweitzer himself, both for being the man he is and for having written so fully of his own thoughts and experiences. I am also in debt to Brit Kristiansen for her firsthand account of the Nobel Reception in Norway, to Karen Clark for her help in translation, to Dr. F. W. Norwood for his personal account of Albert Schweitzer's visit to London and to Angus Cameron for the use of his Schweitzer library. I am grateful to Charles R. Joy, who has known Albert Schweitzer intimately, for the use of the photo taken at the African hospital, to Berit Bjornstad and Bjorn Fjortoft for their permission to use the photos of the meeting with students in Oslo, and to Yusaf Karsh for the use of his portrait of the Doctor. Finally I wish to thank those people who gave time and thought to the reading of the manuscript. To all of these I am most grateful.

J. B.

Contents

Contents

Photographs

(Following page 66)

Albert Schweitzer

Doctor and Mrs. Schweitzer, in Oslo, after Nobel Prize ceremony, look down on youth parade

Student torch bearers, in Oslo, Norway

A quiet moment in Lambarene

ALBERT SCHWEITZER: MAN OF MERCY

CHAPTER 1

Welcome in Norway

THE time had come. The train from Copenhagen pulled into the Eastend Station at Oslo, in Norway, and a large man, stooped with age, stepped out into the raw, cold November air. The excited murmuring of the crowd rose momentarily and then ceased entirely. Albert Schweitzer, the famous doctor of the African jungle, the man of mercy, carrying his old, familiar, battered, metal suitcase, had come to receive the Nobel Peace Prize. The station was packed with people, rich and poor, old and young, who had gathered to see the man who had given up a life of ease to devote his great talents to the welfare of the natives of Darkest Africa, a man who had received his doctor's degrees in theology, philosophy and music before he even began to study for the medical degree which he was required to secure if he was to serve his fellowmen in the way they most needed. The crowd saw a powerfully built man with a large, untrimmed mustache and unruly hair, now snow white. His eyes were wise and piercing, his smile friendly, and the people were deeply moved. Ap-

1

plause filled the station as he stepped forward to shake hands with everyone who was near.

The welcoming officials of the Nobel Committee, the newspapermen and the photographers were present but these first few moments belonged to the everyday people, who wished to show their love and appreciation to a man who had given himself to the service of others in a way that had caught the imagination of the world. They crowded closer. An old lady pushed forward and placed her hand on his coat and then moved quietly away. Everywhere the shouts of welcome rose and the day seemed brighter.

Finally, the Nobel Prize Committee Chairman took Dr. Schweitzer by one arm and, with the French Ambassador on the honor guest's other side, they turned toward the street. Policemen waved back the crowd to make a passage so that the three could reach the waiting automobile. At the last minute a woman held out a single flower, saying, "Thank you with all my heart." A smartly uniformed chauffeur took the dilapidated suitcase from the visitor's hand and put it into the trunk of the car. The automobile then moved slowly through the crowded streets toward the Grand Hotel, where again people waited and applauded as the doctor stepped from the car, and again there were cries of welcome. On this, his first visit to Norway, Albert Schweitzer was received exactly like an old friend returning home. Right from the first he felt the warm thought and friendship of the Norwegian people and the responsive smile of gratitude did not leave his tired old face during his entire stay.

Later in the same day, Mrs. Schweitzer flew from Zurich, Switzerland, to join her husband in Oslo. Though now very frail, she had been his helpmate during forty-two busy, often difficult years. Even as a young student, she had shared his plans and had given up her career as a social worker in order to train as a nurse so that she could help her husband in his African Adventure.

On November second, 1954, Albert Schweitzer had come to Oslo to receive formally the prize he had been awarded two years before for his contribution to the cause of world peace. The prize money, which amounted to $33,149, had already been sent to him and had long since been spent on corrugated iron and other necessities for a leper hospital, which was a separate enterprise for his Lambaréné hospital in French Equatorial Africa. In 1952, when the award was first made, he was too busy building this hospital to go to Oslo and the prize had been received in his name by the French Ambassador to Norway. But winning the Peace Prize also carries an obligation, which is to deliver a lecture on Peace, in Oslo. So it was that Dr. Schweitzer came to fulfil his part and to speak to the world.

To understand the significance of the honor, we need to know what the Nobel Peace Prize is and why it is given. Alfred Bernhardt Nobel was born in 1833. He became a chemist and engineer, and devoted his life to the study of explosives, including dynamite, in the course of which he accumulated a great fortune. When he died in 1896, he was fully aware of the terrible destructive effects of his inventions when related to warfare, and he left his wealth to be used for prizes intended to reward outstanding efforts on the part of scientists and humanitarians to promote the peace and welfare of mankind. Five Nobel prizes are given every year, for the best contributions in the fields of physics, chemistry, physiology and medicine, literature, and peace. They are open to all nationalities. The Peace Prize itself consists of a gold medal, a diploma describing the achievements of the winner, and a sum of money. In acknowledgment, the recipient must deliver a speech, and Albert Schweitzer had worked on his during every moment he could take away from his hospital duties since he had received the award in 1952.

On arrival at the Grand Hotel, he found his suite filled with flowers, together with a personal greeting from King Haakon VII and an invitation to visit the palace that very day. The thoughtfulness of the Norwegians, of king and people alike, impressed the doctor greatly.

The busy schedule which followed was hard on a man seventy-nine years old and already very tired, but, as usual, his iron will and strength made it possible for him to fulfill each engagement with spirit and enthusiasm. By the second day, the hotel room had taken on his own personality and was already as like his working room at Lambaréné as possible. His secretary sat at a small table, answering in longhand the flood of invitations and writing the thank-you notes for the flowers. The flowers themselves had been sent away to people who could enjoy them, for the doctor found it disturbing to see cut flowers wither

4

and fade away. His reverence for all life was such that even the death of flowers was hurtful to him.

Dr. Schweitzer sat on the hardest chair he could find and went over his address, speaking it half aloud to himself. The telephone bell rang continually and visitors kept on arriving at the door, each receiving his full attention—and each visitor, noting the absence of flowers, then hurried away to make up for the oversight! Bouquet after bouquet arrived, only to meet the disposition of the earlier ones.

Part of the afternoon was taken up by a press conference, during which the doctor answered wisely and seriously the questions put to him and still found time to smile and joke so that his questioners felt at ease with him immediately. He refused, however, to make a nation-wide broadcast, since he does not feel at home with an unseen audience. One journalist inquired, "Dr. Schweitzer, if you could live your life over again, what would you do?" He answered, "If I should live again, I would take the same path, for this is my destiny. My life has not been an easy one. I have had many difficulties. Yet I belong to the privileged few who have been able to follow the ideal of their youth, and I am deeply thankful." Another asked, "What books do you plan to write now?" and received the reply, "There are many things I want to finish. The war has interfered with my writing, but if I keep my health, I will work on the books I have started, the third volume of *The Philosophy of Civilization,* and another—a religious book, and try to finish them. It is my great hope that I may succeed. It will take some time for me to complete the last volume of my book on Civilization, for I do not want to have in it one unnecessary word. All day long at the hospital I long for a moment of leisure when I can be by myself and write, but these moments are rare." When the conference was over, one of the journalists wrote, "He has the kindest eyes in the world."

Dr. Schweitzer grew so tired as the day passed that he could hardly speak, yet when evening came he relaxed and was his usual jovial self as he entertained a few very old friends in his hotel room. The evening was his and he and his companions had great fun at dinner when the fish course arrived for, thinking the menu offered individual servings, each had ordered one, only to be faced by five huge creatures when the waiter brought the food.

In the middle of that cold November night, Eline Andersen and her sister, both young schoolgirls, left their home in the suburbs and, carrying stools and a rucksack containing food, walked all the way to the center of Oslo to take their places near the head of a line already forming to secure tickets for the Nobel Lecture. They started their long wait at exactly two a.m., in the morning of November fifth. Only two hundred tickets were available to the general public and before morning arrived the queue was already far too long. Eline and her sister stood for twenty hours to obtain tickets for a lecture they would be unable to understand, simply because they wanted to see the jungle doctor. A reporter, noticing

Eline near the head of the line, asked her why she was willing to stand so long and received the reply, "Because he is the greatest man who lives today." The phrase was at once picked up by the papers, for it seemed to express what all the people of Norway felt about their visitor. The two hundred tickets were quickly sold and most of the persons went away disappointed, to stand as close to the University Hall as they could, just to catch a glimpse of the great man as he entered.

The lucky ticket holders filled all the seats in the white marble University Festival Hall and many stood at the back. As Dr. and Mrs. Schweitzer and the official committee entered, promptly at 5:15, the audience rose to its feet as one man and applauded as though it would never stop. The doctor was dressed in his somewhat old-fashioned black afternoon coat, wing collar and bow tie, and for once his white hair was perfectly in place, though not for long. While flashlight pictures were being taken, he ran his hands through his hair so that it soon fell forward in its usual characteristic manner. At half past five, the King entered, accompanied by his granddaughter, Princess Astrid, and others of the royal party, to take the special seats set aside for them. With their arrival the meeting started and the speaker was introduced.

Albert Schweitzer walked slowly to the platform, carrying the script for his lecture tied together with the usual bit of string. He put on his glasses and began to read his peace message to the world. For fifty minutes he stood erect and spoke in French before an audience that re-

7

mained perfectly silent, although few could understand. Had he spoken in his native German, most of the Norwegians would have been able to follow him, but because he was officially a representative of France and his hospital is in French Equatorial Africa, he used that language. The speech was not translated as it was delivered and the majority of his audience had to turn to their newspapers the next day to find out the meaning of what they had heard. Yet they had had no trouble in appreciating the kind of man who had stood before them.

"The Problem of Peace in the World Today," which was the title of his speech, held a message for us all. "Man," he said, "has become a superman in control of the forces of nature, yet he has not raised himself to the level of reason corresponding to his strength. Man can make atom bombs capable of destroying the human race, but now he must have the higher purpose of gaining a super reason so that we no longer put to evil uses the great power now at our disposal. Whether we secure a lasting peace depends both upon individuals and upon the nations they compose. Both as individuals and as nations we should reject war because it makes us guilty of the crime of inhumanity. The human spirit in our time is capable of creating a new attitude of mind based on moral principles. May those who have in their hands the fate of nations take to heart the words of the apostle Paul: 'if it be possible, as much as lieth in you, live peaceably with all men.' This applies to nations as well as individuals. May the nations in their efforts to keep peace go to the farthest limits of possibility, so that the spirit of man shall be given time to develop and grow strong—and time to act."

The Oslo visit allowed little time for rest between official meetings. One of these was a talk on tropical medicine to the Medical Society. Such time as was actually set aside for quiet, Dr. Schweitzer spent in the lobby of the hotel, autographing books, among them being six which were to be raffled to raise money for Czech refugee children.

His fame as an organist had also long preceded him, but when he first arrived he said he was much too exhausted to give an organ recital and those who had hoped to hear him as a great musician were disappointed. Yet the temptation to try out a new simplified organ invented by an Oslo musician was so great that he visited Trinity Church to find out what it was like. Only the handful of people in his party were fortunate enough to hear his brief recital of Bach's music. However, once he had played on the new organ, he went to the cathedral to play the great organ there and word of this got around sufficiently in time for at least a few music lovers to hear Bach played by a master organist.

The youth of the city wished to pay homage to the great Doctor Schweitzer, as well as to have all of Oslo meet him insofar as this was possible, so the Student Society arranged a meeting in the beautiful City Hall. Here the Student President made Doctor Schweitzer an honorary member of the Norwegian Student Association. To the presentation speech, which the student delivered in French, Dr. Schweitzer replied, "I am deeply touched by what the Norwegian youth have done for me and I will take all these memories with me back to the Jungle."

The students were meeting in the City Hall, and, Kari, Mette and Kristian Kristiansen hurried along the brightly lighted Karl Johann Strasse. They were joined by their friends and together they ran through the crowds, threading their way toward University Square where already hundreds of students stood waiting with flaming torches. The Kristiansens and their friends were given their own torches, which they lighted from others around them and then moved on immediately to take part in the torchlight parade of two thousand high school and university students marching toward City Hall. The night was dark and windy and the flames blazed high. When they reached the open square in front of the hall, the crowd within had already mingled with the ten thousand waiting in the square. All kept their eyes on the balcony of the City Hall, tense with a happy, joyful anticipation that only youth can show.

They had not long to wait before the Student President opened the doors and Dr. and Mrs. Schweitzer stepped out onto the windy balcony. The crowd in the Square went wild. The old couple and the young man stood still, looking down into the sea of faces lighted by the

10

flaring torches. Here was youth, the torchbearers of the new day, ready to carry the light forward from the man who had not been satisfied with words alone but had put those words into action. The Student President called, "Look at him, learn from him," and then, spontaneously within the crowd, the song rose in response, with its triumphant beginning—

"Fight for everything you love,
Die if so you must."

With tears in his eyes, Albert Schweitzer looked into their glowing faces and heard the stirring words of the song. "The memory of this evening will give me strength to carry on—a thousand thanks, *Auf Wiedersehen.*" And the crowd answered, "Auf Wiedersehen!"

The torches were extinguished. The moment had passed. The young people moved away down the street and returned to their homes. But for Kari and Mette and Kristian and all their student friends the memory will linger always in their hearts.

Early in the visit, a newspaperman asked Dr. Schweitzer what he intended to do with the Nobel Prize money. The doctor laughed and said he had already used it to start his leper hospital in Africa. "But," he added, "much more is needed to finish it." This was enough to give the editor of one of the Norwegian papers an idea which spread over the entire country. He suggested that people wishing to contribute to a fund for the leper hospital should send donations to their local newspaper offices. So it came about that on Saturday morning, only four days after his arrival, Dr. Schweitzer was presented with a check for $35,000—considerably more than the amount of the original Nobel Prize money. This was a gift from the hearts of the people, and now the great doctor was anxious to speak to them over the radio. He needed to thank them.

People on the streets were stopped and asked, "What would you do if you met Albert Schweitzer?" The first said, "I should bow down in the dust. Among human beings he stands as number one." The second said, "I have not read his books, but this is not necessary since the greatness of the man consists in the fact that he has made himself known by his deeds." The third said, "Isn't it strange that the whole world is surprised when a man does exactly what all of us ought to do?" Said the fourth person, "If more of his spirit were in the world, everything would be right." And yet another said, "He is the great man of the people in a troubled world. His unselfishness is unequalled in our time." All were right, for Albert Schweitzer has become a living legend.

Saturday evening the doctor's all-too-short visit in Norway came to an end and once again the station was filled with people who had come to pay a last tribute to a man who had won their hearts. And once again a song broke forth:

> "Lovely is the Earth
> Stately is the Heaven
> Beautiful the pilgrimage of the Soul."

12

The old man listened until they had finished and then he said, "The next time you sing that song, send me a friendly thought." He boarded the train, but would not allow the window to be closed, for he did not want to be cut off from his friends. . . . "Such things as this are experienced only once." The crowd watched his erect figure as the train drew slowly out of the station. They could see his smile, but they knew his eyes, like theirs, were filled with tears.

CHAPTER 2

Early Childhood

ALBERT SCHWEITZER was born on the fourteenth of January, 1875, in the little town of Kaysersberg, in Alsace, that rich land bordering the west bank of the Rhine and claimed by both France and Germany. His father was minister to a small Evangelical Church there. The house in which he was born has survived the bombings of two world wars and looks much the same as it did at the time of his birth. Even the country around is little changed. Grape vines still cover the hillsides as they did in 1875, which was outstanding as a year for good wines, because the vines hung particularly heavy with fruit and the grapes brought prosperity to the valley.

Albert was the second child, his sister Louise having been born the year before. He was sickly from the beginning, being so thin and weak and having such a small spark of life at first that his mother and father feared their baby was dead. When he was six months old, his young parents moved to Günsbach, where his father became pastor of the village church. The move was a happy one, for Günsbach was close to his mother's old home at Mühlbach, where her father was minister, so it was like a home-coming to her.

When the day arrived for Albert's father to present himself, together with his family, to his new congregation, Albert's mother dressed the children in their best clothes, lace and ruffles for Louise and a long soft linen dress with bows of ribbon for her sickly baby son. The wives of the pastors of all the churches in the valley came to the house to shake hands with the new minister and his wife and to speak to pretty little Louise, standing at their side. Not one of them even mentioned the thin baby, yellow-faced with jaundice. They just looked at him and, lacking any words to hide their embarrassment, hurried on. At last the young mother could stand the silent inspection no longer and she ran with her baby to her room and wept over him. It was a weak start for one who was to become so strong both in body and spirit.

Rich, thick milk from a neighbor's cow and the good fresh air and summer sun worked wonders. By the time Albert was two years old he was sturdy and healthy, and here in the home at Günsbach, together with Louise and two younger sisters and a brother, he spent a happy childhood. Strong muscles came from racing across the fields of Münster Valley, and from climbing the foothills of the Vosges Mountains, following the riverlets to their sources. The children had love and security and the great outdoors built into them from the very start.

Each Sunday morning the small Schweitzer children,

dressed in their Sunday clothes, were taken to church by the family servant girl, who sat with them to keep them from squirming about too much while their father preached. The service was long and tedious for Albert, who was but three or four, and again and again the maid's cotton gloved hand was placed over his mouth to hide his yawn or to muffle his voice when, with youthful enthusiasm, he sang too loud.

Yet he loved to go to the church and was fascinated by a shaggy, whiskered face which appeared in a bright mirrored frame at the side of the organ. The face twisted and turned continually while the organ played and the congregation sang, but it disappeared as if by magic as soon as his father stood up to preach. For a long time the boy was completely puzzled, but finally his young mind solved the problem to his own satisfaction—it was the devil, who looked down upon all the people in the church. As soon as his father began to speak the words of God, the devil had to leave in a hurry. But the minute the sermon was over and his father sat down again, the devil returned to watch the congregation as they sang the closing hymn. Not until years later, when Albert was a schoolboy, did he realize that the face was only the reflection of the organist and that the man left his seat at the instrument during the sermon.

Like many of the townspeople of Günsbach, Pastor Schweitzer kept beehives in his own backyard, periodically robbing the bees of their honey for the benefit of his family. Albert, still young enough to be wearing the petticoats which were the fashion for small boys in those days, stood on a stool to watch his father tend the bees. A bee settled on the back of his hand and, as he watched it in delighted fascination, it stung him. The shriek that followed brought his frightened mother and the servant girl running from the house, and the attention, the kisses and the comforting that followed were so gratifying that he cried all the louder. The pain was gone long before he stopped and for days afterward he had a miserable, conscience-stricken feeling from having prolonged and exaggerated the incident. The memory of it stayed with him through his later years, causing him to make light of any misfortunes which came his way.

Because the village was small, Albert was in reality a country boy, and, like all children, he loved animals, particularly those he knew on the farms. To herd sheep, cows and pigs was as pleasant an occupation as a boy could have and he decided to be a swineherd when he grew up. Driving the cows to the high summer pastures and returning with them in the fall was exciting even to think about and this was one of his earliest ambitions. Always there were chickens, ducks, kittens and, of course, a dog in the Schweitzer yard, and it was fun for a small boy to harness the dog to a little cart and ride around the garden, or to race with a pup across the open fields to the river. It came as a shock to the sensitive nature of the boy to realize that all animals are not cared for and loved, and that some are actually mistreated. Once when he was taken to the near-by town of Colmar he saw a lame old horse

17

lying on the ground. It was being yanked by one man and beaten by another, only to be carted at last to the slaughterhouse. The scene haunted and tormented him for weeks, and this perhaps was the real awakening of Albert Schweitzer to all the pain and misery in the world.

During these years before his schooldays began, Albert came to the conclusion that it was unreasonable to pray for men every night and leave out God's other creatures, so when his mother had heard his prayers and kissed him good night he added another prayer of his own, young as he was, for all living things—"Dear God, guard and bless everything that breathes; keep it all from evil and give it quiet sleep."

Apart from this dawning sensitivity and reaction to the misery in the world, the only flaw in his otherwise happy childhood was the terror inspired by the sacristan and gravedigger Jägle, who possessed a sense of fun which Albert could not appreciate. His humor took the form of teasing in a terrifying way, for after he had rung the church bell on Sunday morning, he came to the house to talk to Pastor Schweitzer about the other details of the morning service and always managed to place his hands on the small boy's forehead and to say, "Yes, the horns are growing!" It just happened that Albert did have a pair of rather prominent bulges on his forehead, and so, after seeing a picture of Moses with horns, he lived in fear that he himself would one day sprout them too. When Sunday came he longed to run away and hide but did not have the power, for he seemed drawn toward Jägle, to hear the fatal words that at last the horns were breaking through the skin. For nearly a year the thought tormented him, until at last he told his worries to his father and was greatly relieved to hear that his fears were unfounded. So for a time the sacristan had no hold over him, but one Sunday morning the man looked at the boy as if judging his size and said, "Well, Albert, you are growing up so fast it won't be long until you are a soldier. You'll soon be having the blacksmith measure you for your iron soldier suit." The boy's eyes widened. "Do soldiers wear iron clothes?" he asked. "Oh yes! Since Prussia has owned Alsace, all our own soldiers have to wear iron clothes." The sacristan walked on into the house, but he had planted fresh seeds of fear in the child's mind and each day Albert spent some time in front of the blacksmith's shop, watching for soldiers to come to be measured, but no one came. Long afterward, he happened to be standing with his mother before a picture of a mounted soldier wearing armor and he asked, "Will I wear a suit of iron clothes when I am a soldier?" "No, of course not. Common soldiers wear cloth uniforms," was the reply, much to his relief, because he knew that he would never be more than a common soldier and so could forget the iron suit.

Albert did not look forward to going to school. Somehow he knew that then his time for dreaming and his unlimited freedom would come to an end. Nevertheless, one bright October day, his father tucked a new slate under Albert's arm and took him down to the village school, and in spite of tears and red eyes and muffled

19

sobs, the small boy was handed over to the schoolmistress.

To many people the grass always grows greener over the hill but Albert Schweitzer has constantly seen things clearly for what they are. And so on this first day of school, he was reluctant to let go of the life he valued for a different one that he might or might not like.

Yet new and exciting experiences always stand out vividly as memories, and such were his early visits to Colmar. Perhaps you yourself can remember your first impression of a city with its crowds, its noises, and its bright lights. When Albert went to visit his godmother at Colmar he had experiences he had never even dreamed of. There were the trips to the museum to see the art collection, of which the city was very proud. Here he discovered the paintings by the famous German artist, Grünewald, which were hung in a badly lighted corner where most visitors, including his family, passed them by. One of the paintings attracted him in a strange way and he often lingered in front of it until he was fetched. The brilliant colors and the realism of all the paintings fascinated him, for he felt he could almost step into a frame and pick up the familiar articles. The picture that caught his eye most was a representation of the place in which Jesus was born. This included a wooden tub, used as a baby's bath, exactly like the one he and his sisters and brothers had been bathed in.

The paintings of animals and of the face of the devil he thought were exactly as they should be, but above all he was fascinated by the hair on the head of the Apostle John, for the tousled mop of straw-colored hair was exactly like his own. He pitied John and wondered if he too had suffered from the brushing and combing required whenever it had to be put in order. Albert could still feel how it had hurt when the servant girl that very morning had brushed and combed and even brilliantined his hair to make it lie flat. An hour later, as usual, no parting could be seen and only the soreness of his scalp reminded him that his hair had once been combed, plus the girl's voice still ringing in his ears with, "You can tell your character by the way your hair grows—unruly within, unruly without!" Here was St. John the Apostle with the same head of hair and obviously his hair had not kept him from becoming one of the Apostles. So one more fear was left behind, and now, after his eightieth birthday, that unruly thatch still falls over the doctor's eyes but without troubling him, for what was good enough for St. John is good enough for Albert Schweitzer.

It was in Colmar that Albert saw his first fair and took part in the country dances, and although you could hardly call it voluntary on his part, the experience was indeed a memorable one.

Godmother Barth's parting words to her two maids were, "You can take Albert for a walk, only a short one, mind you, and be sure to watch him carefully all the time." Hardly had she gone on an errand of her own than the maids put on their best clothes and started down the road toward Horbourg, with young Albert between them. Before long they heard a band and soon joined the colorful and noisy crowd at the Horbourg Fair. Such in fact had been their intention from the first, for they were smitten by two young men who were waiting to take them on the floor for the country dances. All the time one maid held Albert's right hand and the other the left, while each swain linked arms with his girl on the other side. For the whole afternoon the small boy was swept back and forth in the middle of the group, as completely forgotten as was the passing time. Then it became necessary to run back along the road in order to get home before the mistress returned.

Before they arrived the girls said, "There's no need to say we've been to the fair, Albert!" Fortunately, for the thought of having to tell a lie was like a shadow, all his godmother said was, "Nice, was it?" taking his rosy face and sparkling eyes to be the result of a walk in the country. His guilty secret, however, was soon put in the shadow by another and a greater one. In his new adventure, as with the first, he himself was not in control, although that did not save him from the punishment which eventually overtook him.

One lovely afternoon, young Albert was entrusted to the care of a boy only a couple of years older, the son of a friend of both his mother and godmother. Of course Godmother Barth gave the older boy many instructions—"Don't go to the Lauch river and, above all, you must not go boating. You'll look after him properly, won't you?" The boy was more developed than Albert and seemed quite at home wandering along the narrow streets on the way out of town. Albert was highly excited because he had not been in this part of Colmar before and it was all new to him. Finally the pair reached the banks of the river and the younger boy could hardly contain himself, for it was larger than any he had seen before and had real boats on it, filled with vegetables and each steered by a man in the stern. Albert had already changed from wanting to be a swineherd to wishing to be a coachman and later a pastry cook, but recently he had decided to be a sailor. Here at last was the real thing, or almost, and his mother's disturbing statement that a sailor always slept in a hammock instead of a bed was all but forgotten, for here was the life he wanted. The two boys wandered along the shore, entranced by the noise and excitement.

"Let's find one not tied up properly," said the older boy, and Albert, hardly believing his eyes, saw him untie a boat and jump aboard.

"Come on, get in," he called.

"Oh, no, remember what Godmother said," replied Albert, holding back.

"Better get in before it moves away," came the shout.

"We mustn't do it! Remember what my godmother said!" Albert begged. And then, because he had to choose between being left on a strange riverbank or get into the moving boat, he jumped aboard. His remorse was short-lived, for now he was drifting down the river in a boat for the first time in his young life. This was no dream but something that was really happening! All around them were other boats, taking vegetables to market. His companion was so obviously at home, it was easy to see this was not the first time he had ventured on the water. They skimmed quietly along under the low-hanging trees until they heard angry voices in the distance behind them, upon which the youthful skipper skilfully turned the boat about, explaining, "We had better be going back." Already they could see the owner of the boat, standing on the bank in a terrible rage, and as they jumped ashore they heard him call, "I'll tell your mother this time!" And he did.

When Albert was taken back home to Günsbach, his mother asked as usual whether he had been a good boy and he heard his godmother answer, "Not altogether." Then she went on to tell the story of the river exploit. And although she was careful to explain that he had been influenced by an older boy, he was punished as if he alone had been responsible. Somehow it didn't seem to matter too much, for he had been in a boat on the river and would never forget it.

For the most part, Albert became a quiet boy, much given to dreaming. He even had some trouble learning to read and write, perhaps because his thoughts still dwelt on the pleasures of the carefree life he had so recently left behind him. Living in his dream world, however, did not keep him from checking the school mistress whenever he felt she wasn't telling a story as it should be.

Being a son of the pastor, Albert was already very familiar with Bible stories. The summer before he entered school, during a very rainy spell, he remarked to his father, "It must have been raining for forty days and forty nights and the water still isn't up to the house, much less the top of the mountains!"—to which his father answered, "The great flood wasn't at all like this rain. In the beginning of the world, rain didn't come down in small drops but more as if you were pouring water out of a bucket." So when the schoolteacher told the class the story of the Flood, Albert waited eagerly for the important part, where she would explain the difference between the way it rained in those days and the way it rained now. When she finished without even mentioning the nature of the rain, he could stand it no longer and cried out, "But you must tell the story correctly! You must say that in the days of the flood it didn't rain in drops but like water pouring from a bucket." Only the teacher knew what she felt about this outburst! No matter how far off in his dreams young Albert seemed to be, he was never caught when questions were asked.

Before Albert Schweitzer was old enough to go to school, his father had already started to give him music lessons on an old square piano which his mother had inherited from her father, Albert's grandfather Schillinger. The boy's own father was no great musician and lacked technical skill, but he did have the ability to improvise and very soon Albert was able to play all the hymn tunes, using his own accompaniment, for he found he much preferred to invent harmony than stick to the actual notes.

When Albert was seven he began to find his singing teacher's habit of playing a tune with one finger and with no accompaniment far from pleasing. One day, during a pause when she rose from the harmonium, he asked, "Why don't you play it properly with harmony?" He didn't notice whether she was embarrassed or not but, in his enthusiasm, sat down at the instrument and played the tune in a several part harmony of his own invention. The teacher was impressed and thereafter she looked at him with a new, though still friendly expression, on her face—although she still picked out the tune with just one finger! Albert realized then that he had unintentionally showed off in a way that she was unable to match and so he may have humiliated her before the class. He had taken it for granted until now that everyone could harmonize and, for the first time, it dawned upon him that talent is not evenly distributed to all alike.

Those first lessons he received from his father were the beginning of a musical experience which was to continue all his life and bring him, as Albert Schweitzer the musician, on to the concert stage in the more important cities of Europe. Music had power over him from the start. When he was seven, he arrived too early for a penmanship lesson one day and had to wait outside in the hall. He heard a class inside begin to sing in two-part harmony, *Beautiful forest, who planted you there?* He found this so thrilling that he had to lean against the wall to support himself. And at a later time, when he heard his first orchestra concert and the way the brass instruments played together, his pleasure was so intense he almost fainted.

Albert had inherited more from his grandfather Schillinger than the old piano. He probably received his passion for playing the organ from this gentleman, too. He never knew him in person but his mother often told him tales of his grandfather's love for organ music. The man was interested not only in playing and improvising on the organ but in every detail of its construction. At one time when a famous organ was being built at Lucerne, in Switzerland, he journeyed there and spent days inside the church, watching Herr Haas, the organ-builder, at work. When it was finally finished, he was able to test its perfection. Indeed, whenever Pastor Schillinger visited a strange town, he went first to inspect and try out the organ in the church there. No wonder Albert could hardly wait until his own legs would be long enough to reach the pedals and to have the organist show him how to use the stops in the organ loft of the church at Günsbach. The man whose face he had first seen reflected in the mirror and whom he had mistaken for the devil was now to open a new world to the lad who one day would be known, not only as one of the greatest of organ players, but also as a foremost authority on organ construction.

At the age of nine, the organist allowed Albert to take his place during the morning service in the Günsbach Church, but he had to become a grown man before he learned how to take apart and clean an organ. Once he was able to take down and put an organ together again, he rarely missed an opportunity to do so. Many years later, a tall man covered with dirt and grease was seen working late one night in the organ loft of a church in Switzerland, and it was with much surprise that he was recognized some days afterwards as the artist who was about

27

to give an organ concert for a large and enthusiastic audience—as Albert Schweitzer, the great musician.

He may have inherited still more than a piano and a
love of music from his mother's father. Both Albert and
his mother had the grandfather's same quick temper! This
was a decided liability, for Albert found his temper hard
to control and once, when he was nine, he struck his sister
Adele simply because she was not putting her heart into
a game they were playing. He always played with great
earnestness and easy winning and lack of opposition an-
gered him. The solution was by no means easy. In order
to keep control of himself, even though he was a boy of
nine, with all a boy's enthusiasm for strenuous games, he
gradually began to stop playing games. It was more important to become master of himself than to play too hard
and lose his temper.

Albert also inherited from his mother a certain shyness
and reserve which formed a close bond between them,
although their shyness prevented them from talking openly
to one another when they were together. His grandfather
Schillinger had a very different character. Albert's mother
often told her children stories about her father and young
Albert was fascinated by the man who was so interested in
what went on in the world that, after his Sunday service
was over, he held a crowd about him out in the street,
while he explained the political news and discoveries and
inventions of the times. If the heavens held anything unusual, he set up a telescope in his garden so that anyone
could come and have a look. Pastor Schillinger was a

great friend of the Catholic Vicar and when it was necessary for either man to be out of the village for a few days, the other visited the sick and the shut-ins of both Catholic and Evangelical alike. Yet the same friendly Pastor Schillinger insisted that any man who wished to see him in his study must come respectfully dressed, wearing a black coat and tall hat.

His mother told Albert that all day Saturday her father worked on his sermon for the next morning and the house had to be absolutely quiet—not a sound could be made by anyone. When his Uncle Albert, for whom he had been named was a boy he was never allowed even to come home from school on a Saturday holiday for fear he would disturb his father's work on the weekly sermon. Young Albert's mother loved her brother very much, so that he became a special hero to her, and her son was afraid he would never live up to his fine name. The story of his uncle's greatest deed of heroism was a favorite one which he often heard. Uncle Albert had been a pastor in Strasbourg and in the year 1870, after the battle of Weissenburg, he went to Paris to obtain medical supplies and other necessities because the inhabitants of Strasbourg expected to be besieged any day. This errand took a long time because of the red tape involved in getting even the small number of things he wanted, so when he was ready to return, he was stopped by the commander of the besieging army and made a prisoner. He was allowed to send the supplies through to Strasbourg, but he was tormented by the thought that his people had to withstand the siege without his help, as well as by the fear that they might think he had deserted them in their time of need. He died two years later, from the after-effects of his imprisonment, and it was only natural that young Albert, who now bore his uncle's name, should feel that he was expected to carry on the brave life which had been so tragically cut short.

CHAPTER 3

A Village Schoolboy

WHEN Albert went to school he wanted more than anything to be accepted by his schoolmates as one of them. They were all peasant boys while he was the pastor's son, which at once set him apart as one of the gentry. Every time there was a dispute, the boys of the village school taunted him with the cry, "sprig of the gentry," although they accepted without comment all his efforts to close the economic and educational gap between them.

One day, on the way home from school, he and a schoolmate, George Nitschelm, had a friendly tussle, for like all boys, Albert found pleasure in measuring his strength with others in play. George was the larger and so it was with some surprise that Albert found he could get him down and sit on him. Tired from the struggle, yet pleased to learn that he was becoming so strong, he laughed happily as he allowed George to get to his feet. George, however, was not laughing. "If I got broth to eat twice a week as you do, I'd be as strong as you are!" he exclaimed. It was what all the boys felt. The realization that they thought him better off than they hurt Albert deeply, for he felt himself to be no different and it wasn't his fault he was the son of the pastor. For a long time afterward the sight of broth made him feel sick, because George's words still rang in his ears and with each swallow he felt he was about to choke.

It was important to belong to the group. Albert was determined to be exactly like the other boys at school and since they had fingerless gloves, so did he. He refused to wear leather shoes during the week and would use only the wooden clogs worn by the peasant children. Sunday was the only day on which the other boys put on their boots, and so it was with Albert, too.

When cold winter weather arrived and an old overcoat of his father's was cut down to fit and the tailor, pleased with a job well done, remarked, "Now you are a regular gentleman!" Albert at once made up his mind not to let any of the boys see him wearing it. Occasionally, in the privacy of his home, Albert was required to dress "to fit his position," in order to please his parents, for they did not at all understand his "peculiar" attitude. So, when guests came to dinner, rather than hurt his mother and father, whom he loved very much, he quietly put on his shoes.

An overcoat was different because it was something to be worn only outdoors and when the next cold Sunday came, he refused to wear it to church. His father became angry and boxed his ears, but still Albert refused. Even being whipped and locked in the cellar failed to alter his stubborn determination. When he had to choose between the ridicule of the village boys and displeasing his father, the hurt looks and punishment he received from his parents were easier to bear than that dreadful "sprig of the gentry."

Once when Albert's mother took him on a visit to Strasbourg, they went into a shop to buy a much needed hat. The boy objected to every hat his mother or the shopkeeper placed on his head, and when they agreed on a sailor's cap, Albert protested so violently that everyone in the store came over to see what was happening. Finally the shopkeeper asked, "What kind of a cap *do* you want, you stupid boy?" Albert replied between sobs, "I want one like the village boys wear." Out of the unsaleable stock just such a cap was found for him, a brown one which could be pulled down over the ears. He hated to embarrass his mother but he was pleased with his cap, for it looked like anything but a "young gentleman's new-fashioned hat." He had a feeling, however, that this time his mother understood and it gave him a warmth inside, for it was not his nature to be stubborn or disagreeable.

Albert also felt compelled to act as well as look like the village children. On one occasion he joined the schoolboys when they ran shouting after a donkey cart driven by a Jew named Mausche. The quiet little man bought and sold land and cattle and sometimes found it necessary to pass through the village of Günsbach. There were no other Jews in the neighborhood and the boys always ran after the cart, jeering at him and calling out names as they followed him out of the village.

One of these times, when they reached the bridge, the Jew turned and gave the boys a gentle and somewhat embarrassed smile. Albert saw the smile, understood what it meant to remain silent, even when persecuted, and never jeered again. After that experience, he always greeted the man politely, and as he grew a little older, he always shook hands with the Jew and walked a little way by the side of the cart, talking with him in friendly fashion. Mausche never knew that his smile taught Albert Schweitzer one of the greatest lessons of his life, that of tolerance.

The time came finally when Albert Schweitzer was to free himself from the fear of being laughed at by his school friends whenever he did not agree with them. It began one bright spring Sunday morning, the week before Easter, when he was seven or eight years old.

For the past week Albert and a small friend, one Henry Bräsch, had been playing with slingshots made out of strips of rubber and string. Hurling pebbles at gate posts and trees was fun. Then early Sunday morning Henry suggested, "Come on, let's go shoot birds!" Albert was horrified but he was afraid to refuse because he feared Henry would laugh at him and tell the other boys. So the two of them went to the still leafless woods where the first spring visitors were hopping about among the branches and filling the air with song. Henry crouched down and placed a stone in his sling and, after a moment's hesitation, Albert did the same and drew it back ready to shoot. At that moment the half-hour warning bell began to ring from the church, calling Christians to worship, and to Albert it seemed like a voice from heaven crying, "Thou shalt not kill." He shouted and threw down his sling, scattering the birds in all directions, then ran home as fast as he could. Since that day, whenever the church bells ring at Easter time and only birds decorate the leafless trees, Albert Schweitzer remembers the bell that rang in his heart that Sunday morning and held him back from destroying such beauty, for here began his reverence for life which was to play such an important part in his future thoughts and actions.

The Schweitzer children owned a dog named Phylax. He was a good playmate but for some reason could not stand the sight of a uniform and always attacked the postman. Since the dog had already tried to bite a policeman, Albert was told that it was his duty to watch Phylax so that there would be no more trouble. This made him a proud animal tamer and when the postman appeared on his rounds he drove Phylax to a corner of the garden where he stood over the barking creature, giving him a blow with a stick whenever he tried to get out.

Later, when the postman had passed and he sat on the steps with the dog, he no longer felt proud of being a "lion tamer." Instead, he was ashamed, for deep in his heart he knew that all he needed to do was to have taken his animal friend by the collar and stroked him in order to keep him from attacking the postman.

Occasionally Albert was allowed to drive a neighbor's

horse and the temptation to whip him into a trot was too great to be overcome. Only when he saw how hot the horse became did he feel sorry and then, looking into the tired eyes of the animal, he silently begged for forgiveness. Going to the river with the other boys to fish also made him miserable, almost to the extent of being ill, when he saw worms being pushed onto barbed hooks and the torn mouths of the fish. Not even the fear of being laughed at by his companions was as unpleasant as the sick feeling he got.

Yet out of such experiences as these, often accompanied by shame, grew the strong belief that it is wrong needlessly to bring pain or death to any living creature. Slowly he lost his fear of being laughed at because he dared to be different, although to be different was never what he wanted.

One day during school recess the boys were told that a large wheel "racer" was standing outside the village inn. For a long time they had all wanted to see one of these newfangled bicycles, because the local wagon drivers had often described how people in the cities raced about on wheels, frightening the horses. School was immediately forgotten and the boys all ran down to the inn. There stood the high-wheel and the children as well as the village grownups stood gaping at it until the owner had finished his glass of wine. When at last he came out of the inn, dressed in knee pants, and mounted the bicycle and rode off, the boys laughed, for they had never seen anything so funny before.

Soon the large wheel bicycles became commonplace and when eventually the smaller ones came into more general use, people made fun of their riders because they thought they were afraid to manipulate the machines with the big wheels. Albert himself bought one of the newer kind, after a few years, with money he earned by teaching mathematics to backward students. A pastor's son was not supposed to ride around on a machine but his father was broadminded and ignored any criticism he heard. This wise man must have realized just how much a bicycle meant to his son, for on it Albert could get far into the countryside in a few minutes and lose himself in the world of nature.

Albert's father was rarely strict with his children. During the many hours he spent each day in his book-lined study, writing or reading, they were entirely free. They loved this freedom and also the summer days when he put aside his work and went with them on long walks into the hills. He had such a vast knowledge of the "whys" of nature that these walks were memorable.

Yet Albert always hated to step into his father's study. He disliked the smell of books and the scratching noise of his father's pen. He vowed he would never be a student and write and study as his father did. Albert and his sisters and brothers, however, dreaded the study for an entirely different reason—they spent some of the most disagreeable hours of their lives there, Albert especially.

Each year, between Christmas and New Year's, there came a day when their father announced at the breakfast table that, immediately after the meal, they were all to come to the study to write their thank-you letters for their Christmas gifts. To Louise, the task was not too bad for she soon had her notes written and was free, but for Albert it was torture and sometimes a whole day passed with only one letter successfully completed. His father sat writing at his desk, while the cries of the village boys could be clearly heard as they played with their sleds on the snow covered hill nearby. Each letter had to contain a sentence of thanks for the gift, a list of all the gifts received, and finish with kind wishes for the New Year. Each letter had to be different and for each a rough copy had to be shown to the father for corrections. When a note was finally passed as perfect, it was copied on good paper, without a single mistake or blot. No wonder that young Albert, on one Christmas morning, began to cry as soon as he opened his gifts, for he realized how great an ordeal was yet to come. Throughout the week before New Year's Day he sobbed all through his meals, but still had to return to the study until all his uncles and aunts and godparents had been thanked.

Today, of course, Schweitzer writes hundreds of letters a year, yet he still finds it hard to compose a letter which has to end with good wishes for the New Year. And when he presents a gift to some small child in his capacity of uncle, godfather or grandparent, he forbids the child to write a letter of thanks, for nothing has ever blotted out the memory of those days of torture in his father's study.

When Albert Schweitzer became a man he was always

thankful for those few years in the village school where
learned that peasant children in wooden clogs can b.
superior in many ways to the more educated children of
the gentry. He always remembered the village boy who
could do mental arithmetic faster than he could, and another who was brighter in geography and yet another who
never forgot a date in history. Albert was young when he
learned what democracy really means, and he learned it
from poor boys with darned stockings and fingerless gloves.

Albert Schweitzer has never outgrown his love for the
village church at Günsbach and it is hardly possible to
overestimate the part it has played in forming his character. He learned in that church to appreciate the need
for solemnity and quiet, and as a grown man feels strongly
that children should be allowed to share in grown-up
religious services, not for what they might understand of
the minister's spoken words but in order to feel something
of what it means to be quiet and serious and solemn.

Albert loved Sunday. He loved the sound of church
bells. And when, with his mother and his sisters and his
brothers, he sat listening to the organ music, he felt a
great peace within his mind and body. As he listened to
his father's sermons even his youthful understanding made
him realize that they were sincere and based on life and
experience. But best of all he loved the afternoon services,
which were less formal, for into these were woven stories
about the work of the missionaries as they carried the
teachings of Jesus throughout the world. The stories came
from a book which his father translated from the French.

39

It contained the memoirs of M. Casalis, a missionary in South Africa. They made a great impression on Albert and reminded him of his favorite statue in the town of Colmar. This was the Bruat Monument by Barthold which consisted of a group of figures, each representing the people of a foreign country. One was an African Negro with such a melancholy expression that Albert always felt sad when he looked at it. The figure fascinated him and he visited it every time he went to Colmar. The statue, together with his father's stories, became so much a part of him that later on, when he decided to serve mankind, it was to the Africans of Central Africa that he went.

The Günsbach church building itself was not without its effect on young Albert, for the inside was by no means severe and plain but was decorated with a Catholic chancel, and the beauty of it meant much to the small boy. It did not seem at all strange to have the village church serve both the Protestants and the Catholics, for the building had done so since the reign of Louis XIV of France, two hundred years before. At that time Alsace had become French and Louis, who wished to humble the Protestants, decreed that in all villages where there were at least seven Catholic families the chancel of the village church was to be theirs exclusively, and that Catholic services were to be held in these churches at stated times on Sundays. To this day the church at Günsbach is still used by both religious groups, although the chancel has now been changed

and retains none of the charm it had during Albert's youth.

Albert was completely fascinated by the magnificence of the church, with the gold-colored altar and bright bouquet of artificial flowers, the tall candlesticks, and above the altar the large gilt statues of Mary and Joseph. On a bright Sunday the sun flooded through the windows and turned everything within into radiance. Through the chancel windows Albert could see the hills and there were no limits to hold in his imagination. The beauty, the

41

organ music, his father's voice, combined to give him peace and quiet, while the sharing of the Catholic chancel left him with a toleration for other religions than his own which he has always kept and which is an integral part of his character as a man of mercy.

In the autumn of 1884, Albert was enrolled as a student in the Realschule in Münster. This was a modern school where no Latin or Greek was taught—and so, in addition to his other studies, he had to have private lessons in Latin, which were necessary if he wished to go on to the gymnasium or upper school.

The long quiet walks over the hills to and from school every day, always by himself, drew him closer and closer to the natural world about him. He came to know every change of season, from autumn to winter with the wet leaves falling and the bare branches showing sharp against gray and windy skies, then the sunshine of spring with green buds, spring flowers and songbirds all bursting with the new unfolding, followed by the warm, scented breezes of summer and the deep-shaded lanes. Yet this delight was all too short, for during the holidays, after the first year, his parents decided to send him to the Gymnasium at Mülhausen, in Upper Alsace, and many were the tears Albert shed in secret at the prospect of being torn away from his beloved nature. He had tried to express or capture the beauty of the earth in poetry and painting, but without success. Finally he stopped striving to do so and gave himself up to living through his eyes, soaking in the beauty instead of struggling to reproduce it, feeling the rain on his face, hearing the sounds of bird's songs in his ears, and seeing the colors and light and shades of the landscape.

CHAPTER 4

School Away from Home

WHEN the autumn came in 1885, while Albert was still only ten years old, he left the countryside he loved so well and commenced the second phase of his education, at the Lycée de Mülhausen. His godfather and uncle, Louis Schweitzer, generously took the boy in to live with him and his wife while he attended the Gymnasium, which was the name commonly given to the secondary schools. The small salary Albert's father received as pastor of the church in Günsbach could not be stretched to pay for such an expensive education and Albert was able to receive it only because his uncle gave him his room and board and because the school offered free tuition to a parson's son.

His Uncle Louis and Aunt Sophie were no longer young and they had had no children of their own. The uncle was the Director of the elementary schools of Mülhausen and as such lived in the gloomy official residence in part of the Central School. He and his wife were used to a well regulated life in which every minute was planned and every plan carried out, without any change from day to day.

Meals started and finished on time and after the midday dinner Albert practiced his music until it was time to leave for school again. When evening homework was finished, he once more had to practice his piano music and if he protested, his aunt always said, "You'll never know when you will need your music later on." Of course, she did not realize just how much it would mean to Albert Schweitzer the man, for without it he could not have accomplished what he eventually set out to do.

The discipline and the strictly regulated life seemed hard after the freedom of life in Günsbach, but from the start Albert was very much aware of the affection and kindness of his aunt and uncle, and in later years he became more and more appreciative of what he had learned from them.

Yet he was not happy in his new life, partly because there was little opportunity to get out into the country. He longed to walk over the hills alone from Günsbach to Münster but the only walks he now had were on Sunday afternoons, with his aunt and uncle. He was homesick for the Günsbach church, for after the lovely Catholic chancel, the plainness of the Mülhausen church repelled him. He also missed his father's sermons and the church services, with all the men of the village dressed in black and all the women in their native costumes. Sunday had lost its charm, except for the fact that after the Sunday walk he was allowed to read until ten o'clock. This was a great privilege, for even reading was strictly regulated and the boy who had been free to fill his life with books to his heart's desire now had but one period in the week when he was allowed to open a book that was not part of his schoolwork.

Aunt Sophie also loved to read and did so every day for an hour before dinner and for two hours afterward. She read slowly, so as not to miss the style of the author, and on Sunday, when the three sat around the table sharing the same lamp, she knitted and read at the same time. Albert could tell by the speed of the needles whether the style was particularly beautiful, for then the needles almost stopped moving.

On the other hand, Albert read rapidly. He skimmed a book first and if he liked it, then read it carefully, though quickly. To Aunt Sophie this was improper and not the way to read a book at all. She often tried to change his reading habits, but without success.

"It is a disgrace to devour a book like that! You can't be getting a thing out of it," she remarked frequently. "It's no use reading when you miss the style."

Albert would have liked to have said that he didn't miss anything, not even a word, if the style was good. If it wasn't good, he skipped the uninteresting parts and went on to the better. He kept silent, however, for in her power lay his chances of reading at all. She could add a few precious minutes to his reading time or take them away. So he kept still in order not to irritate her and dreaded the passing of time, for at exactly half-past ten she put a marker in her place and closed her book.

When Albert was home from school, he was either practicing at the piano or doing his homework at the dining room table, except for the fifteen minutes just before supper, when the table had to be set. These precious moments were spent reading the daily paper for, like his mother, he kept up with the history of the day by reading the newspaper, and although he was not very old, he had developed a capacity for understanding the politics he read about. Day after day his aunt would take the paper from him, saying, "You are reading the trash in that Literary Supplement. Nothing good can come from reading about murder cases. I forbid you to read such stuff."

He tried to explain that it was the front section, the one on politics, that he read, because he liked history, but the battle went on until finally Aunt Sophie said to his Uncle Louis, "I can't do anything about this newspaper reading. Albert spends all the time reading the supplement and he had better spend the time on his homework or on the piano."

"But, Uncle," Albert protested, "it is really the history I read, as I always did at home."

"We can easily find out whether the boy is reading politics or murders," said his uncle as they sat down to dinner. Then followed an examination which included such questions as, "Who are the ruling princes in the Balkans?" "Who are the prime ministers of the Balkan States?" "Who were represented in the last three French Cabinets?" . . . and so on. Over the meat and potatoes and through the dessert, the uncle questioned and the boy answered promptly. After that, there was no more argu-

47

ment concerning reading the newspaper and Albert was allowed to continue his reading in the evening, when his lessons were finished. Now he really did have time to include the literary supplement, too! But from then on, his uncle treated him with respect, as though he were already grown up, and discussed the political happenings with him throughout the evening meal.

During his first term at the Gymnasium, Albert seemed unable to do his schoolwork satisfactorily. He was inclined to dream about his old life, instead of listening to the master, and he was still somewhat homesick. Also, in spite of his private instruction in Latin, he had difficulty in keeping up with his class. The school principal finally asked his father to come to Mülhausen, where he was told that, unless Albert showed more ability to learn, the scholarship would have to be given up so that some other more worthy student could fill the place. Perhaps another school would suit him better. Pastor Schweitzer was hurt and worried and asked that his son be given a little more time to settle down, and though Albert expected to be punished, his father showed him only kindness when he talked to him. Even then, the boy did not seem able to free himself from his dreaming or to improve his grades, and his Christmas term report caused his mother to weep all through the holidays. Yet the Easter report, three months later, listed him among the best in the class!

What had happened in this short time? Simply that a new form-master named Dr. Wehmann had changed the boy's life completely.

The new master expected and received the respect of the boys and Albert emerged from his dreaminess with a new attitude toward life. Dr. Wehmann carefully prepared his lessons for each day and when he faced the class, he taught exactly the amount he had planned. He returned exercise books, carefully graded, on the day he promised. All of his actions had a purpose and for the first time Albert saw the value of work properly performed. Quite naturally, he began to model his life after that of the master and soon gained self-confidence when he found that he could do his schoolwork well if he went at it in much the same manner as the master. He sensed Dr. Wehmann's devotion to duty in even the smallest matters, and slowly, as the result of this influence rather than from any form of punishment, Albert's mind grew more and more awake.

Not only had his schoolwork been unsatisfactory but his music as well. Aunt Sophie compelled him to spend at the piano all his hours not needed for homework but he played the music in his music book without paying any attention to time or fingering. He liked improvising and composing his own melodies and made almost no effort to learn the pieces assigned to him by his music teacher, Eugene Münch. Herr Münch was organist at St. Stephen's Church and was an excellent instructor, so it is small wonder that he felt he was wasting his time on a boy who not only came unprepared but who played without any feeling for the music before him. Albert, however, could not bring himself to play with any expression before his music master, for shyness overcame him until, one day, when he was playing a sonata by Mozart, Herr Münch became so angry that he exclaimed, "When a boy has no feeling, I can't give him any! You have no right to have me give you beautiful music when you spoil everything you play. Here is Mendelssohn's *Song Without Words* for this week, but you will ruin it as you have ruined Mozart's *Sonata*."

Somehow this was just the challenge which Albert needed. He would show Herr Münch whether he had feelings or not! For once he practiced on his new piece steadily all week and at the next lesson, not only was he time and note perfect, but he had worked out the fingering and marked it on the music above every note. He had never done such a thing before. When he had finished his exercises and scales he turned to the *Song Without Words* and played it from his soul. The music master said nothing but placed his hands gently and firmly on Albert's shoulders and moved him over. Then he played the music according to his own interpretation. The next week Albert played some Beethoven and the following week he was introduced to Bach. Herr Münch held the key which opened to Albert the whole wonderful world of music, and master and pupil became close friends.

Very soon Albert began having lessons on the great organ at St. Stephen's, a dream he had cherished for a long time but, he had felt that there was little chance of its being realized. The thrill must have been tremendous when he first sat at the organ with three keyboards and sixty-two stops, for the boy had organ music in his blood.

Eugene Münch was amazed at his progress and by the time Albert was sixteen he was trusted by his teacher to play at the Sunday Service and still later to join in his master's recitals. The wonderful friendship ended with the death of Herr Münch in 1898. Albert Schweitzer, although only twenty-three, wrote a small book in French in his teacher's memory. It was published in Mülhausen and so became the first of many books which were to carry Albert Schweitzer's name.

Albert learned many things during his first winter away from home, in addition to an appreciation of order and a sense of duty, yet more than ever he longed to walk across wide fields and to hear birds singing in the still leafless trees. One warm day in March, when the sun had melted the snow, leaving patches of grass already beginning to show green, Albert sat at the table, looking longingly out of the window. He had finished his four o'clock coffee and his unopened books lay in front of him. A year ago, when he was still but nine years old, he would have been on his way home from Münster. In his mind, he could see the old castle on the hill, standing out against the spring sky without any heavy foliage to hide his view, and wave after wave of homesickness came over him.

Aunt Sophie looked at him, finished her ironing quickly, put away the ironing board, took off her apron and said, "Come along, I'll take you for a little walk." At the sound of her voice, Albert started, let go of his dream and began hurriedly to open a book. Then he realized what his aunt had said and he could hardly believe his ears,

51

although she was already putting on her hat. He knew she must have read his mind, and that beneath her strict manner she understood his longings and his needs.

So together they went out and walked on and on, across the Canal where the ice blocks were floating, and into the open country. They hardly spoke to one another. Aunt Sophie did not even once suggest that she should return to prepare supper, or even that it was getting late. From then on their relationship was changed. The boy accepted his aunt's strictness and her rules because he knew her heart. He even learned to like the well-ordered life of his aunt and uncle.

When Albert reached the age of fifteen, he was enrolled in a confirmation class under Pastor Wennagel. The religious instruction was well given but there was no time for questions. Yet questions crowded fast into Albert's mind and without any chance to air them, he closed up and thought his own thoughts. He learned his lessons thoroughly and his instructor had no idea at all as to what was going on behind those steady eyes.

On one point Albert was very clear indeed. He did not agree with Pastor Wennagel in his belief that it was necessary to take all of religion on faith, with a deaf ear turned to reason. He felt that all things, even religion, must be put to the test of reason, and perhaps it was just as well that the pastor did not suspect his pupil's ideas. At the end of weeks of lessons, when the boys were kept in turn after class, to be questioned individually, Albert evaded the questions and refused to let the good man know what sort of turmoil went on within him. Pastor Wennagel was hurt and troubled and dismissed the boy, but he reported to Aunt Sophie that Albert was indifferent to the teachings in the confirmation class.

This was far from being the case, for all through the weeks of instruction, Albert was so affected by the lessons and their solemnity that he was almost ill. One last and beautiful touch was given to this stage in his development, on Palm Sunday, as the procession of young people in the confirmation class left the vestry of the church. Eugene Münch at the organ played *Lift Up Your Heads, O Ye Gates!* from Handel's *Messiah,* and Albert realized that it was in perfect harmony with his thoughts on that impressive day.

All through Albert's childhood there was an ever-present shadow. There was never enough money. His father's salary was small and making it stretch to cover food and clothing for five children was hardly possible, no matter how much his mother tried to economize. In those days, the height of economy was to use vegetable fats in place of good rich butter. They were not made as they are now and Albert's mother always thought that the butter substitutes were responsible for the pastor's stomach ailment. This, together with the shortage of money and finally a prolonged attack of rheumatism which made her husband ill for months, put a load on her which proved almost too much for her to bear.

One morning, shortly before the end of a summer vacation spent at home, his mother said, "Your winter suit must be too small for you this year, for you've grown so tall this summer. You'll need a new one."

Albert, however, was old enough to realize what such an expenditure would mean to his family, so he replied promptly, "Not a bit of it, of course it will be all right. I don't need a new suit." But he did, for he could no longer get into last year's winter suit. There was nothing else to do but to wear his light summer suit all winter and put up with the cold as best he could—as well as the pity of his classmates. His aunt thought the experience would harden him morally and physically, but he suffered greatly, both from the cold and from his hurt pride. Never once did he have any money to spend upon himself. He was able to endure this because he knew that by doing without things he was helping his mother in the only way that he could.

The following year when Albert was fifteen, the shadow of poverty was lightened somewhat and his family moved to a new house with a nice garden. In the sunshine of the new garden his father became well again. A legacy from a distant relative of his mother had eased the financial worries to some extent and Albert at last saw his family enjoy good health and happiness. Within this devoted family community of parents and children, each found security, understanding and freedom. They were all closely united, yet every child was encouraged to stand on his own. This ideal family life they shared with their companions, too, for during the holidays school friends filled the house to overflowing.

Never for a moment did Albert accept this happy youth as a matter of course. He was always intensely aware of it and thought often about the question of happiness. He came to feel that he had no right to take his happiness, or his good health and abundant energy, for granted. But that he must also carry some part of the load of misery he found in the world.

Out of all his experiences, his love for his family and for the world of nature, his appreciation of the difficult struggle his parents had to raise and educate their children, the dependence of one upon the other, the sense of duty and spirit of perfection he found in his teachers, and his awareness that happiness and misery are unequally allotted to human beings, gradually came an understanding of the teaching of Jesus that we must not treat our lives as being for ourselves alone. As he grew more and more aware of his own strength and abundant health and became more conscious of his own happiness and appreciation of beauty, his heart also began to fill with compassion for those who were less fortunate or in pain. Sometimes he felt completely carefree, but even more frequently and more strongly the feeling came over him that his personal strength of body and mind were meant to be shared. His feeling of oneness with all people and all living things grew more intense as he grew older, until at last it governed the whole of his life.

Once he was awakened from his daydreaming by Dr. Wehmann, Albert took his place near the top of the class and held it. He had an immense capacity for work, otherwise he could not have studied his school lessons and music at the same time and attained such a high standard in both.

Languages and mathematics were given a great deal of attention, although they were far from being Albert's strong points. The fact that these subjects were so difficult and made him work so hard gave him a great deal of satisfaction, however, simply because they demanded so much of him. On the other hand, he mastered history with little effort and easily led his class. His love for reading and the background he already possessed concerning political events of the day, were sufficient not only to establish history as his best subject at school but also to open doors which have never since been closed. To this day Albert Schweitzer reads history whenever his busy life allows him the least time for it.

The field of science also became a favorite, particularly chemistry, physics and geology, although Albert was not satisfied with the answers his textbooks gave him. Everything seemed to have a ready-made answer, all things were satisfactorily explained, and nothing was left of the mystery of nature. He found this idea ridiculous! Who could really explain hail, snow, rain and wind? He felt that a snow crystal or a raindrop were beyond explanation. They were miracles, as they remain to this day. As a matter of fact, he began to see miracles everywhere and to dream about their wonder. His dreaming now, instead of interfering with his schoolwork, only quickened his mind, so that he was even more alert.

He could easily have filled all of his time with his music, history and science, and he must have felt too often that his other classes were interruptions, especially those in literature, where poetry was taken apart and analyzed until nothing was left that was poetic and beautiful. Albert felt about a poem much as he did about a snowflake—it could not be explained and if one attempted to do so, there was no poem left.

Albert had always been by nature a shy boy and life with Aunt Sophie only served to make him more so, for she believed that being reserved was a mark of good breeding. She impressed on him that forwardness was a fault and that he should overcome any tendency to express his inward feelings or private opinions. Yet when Albert became sixteen he lost all trace of shyness and went almost to the other extreme, freely expressing his own views to anyone on any subject, challenging accepted beliefs and stating his own whenever possible. The desire to put everything to the test of reason went to his head and during this period of his growth he often embarrassed his family, especially his father. When the Schweitzers had visitors, Albert was made to promise not to act so stupidly every time a discussion arose. Any ordinary dinner conversation could easily end in a stormy battle. His aunt thought him insolent to argue so with adults, as though he were one himself!

At this age Albert really was difficult, but it was only

because he was thinking for himself and seeking information, and he wanted other people to reason things out,
rather than just state an opinion without giving any
thought to it.

Albert Schweitzer has never really grown out of this
phase of his education. He still questions everything and
is intolerant of ignorance, two qualities which are the
essence of youth. Now, in his eighties, his mind retains its
youthfulness, although he has learned to be more tactful,
to know when to stop arguing, when to listen and not to
speak. He still resents, however, the time people spend in
what he feels is useless chatter when they might be enjoying a much more satisfying serious conversation. Today,
when he meets a youth who really wants to discuss a problem, he can be as eager as he was at sixteen and he enters
into the mental battle as though the two were the same
age.

During his days at the Gymnasium, Albert was influenced by many persons, especially those masters who
opened new doors for him. Most of them never knew
how much they gave to him. Some of them he himself did
not appreciate at the time as he did later on. Others he
appreciated at once.

William Deecke, the school principal, had a stiff manner, yet the boys appreciated the fact that he was a scholar
who not only taught Latin and Greek but endeavored to
help the boys become thinking men. They understood this
instinctively and responded accordingly. They were impressed by his friendship with the notables of their world,

with the poets and historians, and realized too that Herr Deecke was himself an authority on Greek inscriptions and Etruscan archaeology. The lessons were all made fascinating by the wealth of background material the professor had at his command. It was from this man that Albert gained his love for wisdom and knowledge which we call philosophy, and today Albert Schweitzer is looked upon as one of the great thinkers of our time.

Albert was too shy to thank many of the people who helped him during his school life, although they may have known of his gratitude without actually hearing it expressed. Others lived long enough to become his friends and to these he opened his heart. He was especially glad to have his Uncle Louis and Aunt Sophie realize how dear they had become to him and how much he appreciated what they had done for him.

Albert spent nine years altogether at the Gymnasium and in June of 1893, when he was eighteen, he prepared to take his school-leaving examinations. He was looking forward to going to the University and already knew what he wanted to do. He wished to continue along the road of philosophy opened to him by Professor Deecke, to study theology as well, and of course to go on with his music, which he never really forgot for a minute.

He passed his written examination none too well and even in his essay Albert, who was usually at the top of his class, received only a mediocre grade. There was but one examination left, a long oral examination for which the class was told to wear black suits. Albert did not own one and he felt it was too much to ask his parents to buy one, or even to give him the money to pay for a pair of pants to go with the black frock coat which he had inherited from a relative of his mother.

Several days before the examination, he asked his uncle, "Would you let me wear your black trousers to my examination?"

Uncle Louis looked up at the boy, now so much taller than himself, and considered. "Do you think they would fit?—Well, perhaps for just this once the size won't matter." Neither of them thought of trying the trousers on before the morning of the examination, and then Albert was shocked to find how short they were! Of course, his uncle was shorter and stouter than he was—but surely there was something he could do. He had to! He found a piece of string and lengthened his braces as far as he could, though still the trousers did not reach to the top of his shoes, while a gap of several inches showed between his waistcoat and trousers, exposing the piece of string. But there was no more time, so he put on his frock coat and hurried to the Gymnasium.

The rest of his classmates were all properly dressed and waiting to enter the examination room when Albert arrived.

"Well, have a look at our Schweitzer." . . . "Albert, you clown!" . . . "Are you actually going in there like that?" . . . "Schweitzer, always ready with a laugh!" And they turned him around. "Anyone got any extra string?" . . . "How about adding a ruffle around each leg?"

60

One boy pulled out the ample seat and said, "Room in here for me, too!" They all laughed until they were bent double and Albert, although terribly embarrassed, had to laugh, too. Then the bell sounded and they had to march in to face their examiners. But all seriousness had gone from the occasion and they could not stop laughing.

At a table in the front of the room sat the masters and the commissioner from Strasbourg, who was to preside over the examination. The masters saw Albert's outfit and smiled, for they understood the reason for the merriment. But the commissioner saw only a group of undisciplined boys, presenting themselves for an examination with an entirely wrong attitude.

"This does not seem a fitting occasion for such behavior. I am here to give the class its final examination but apparently you feel it is a time for fun making. Perhaps by the end of the session you will have a very different point of view. You! What is your name?" he called to Albert, for he could see that he was the center of the disturbance.

"Schweitzer, sir. Albert Schweitzer," replied the red-faced youth.

"I will examine this buffoon myself. Perhaps he will not be so conceited when we finish."

Then followed a grilling, the like of which the boy had never even dreamed about. The examiner asked questions in detail about subjects Albert had never heard of and many had to go unanswered. Each time the man would shake his head solemnly. Albert did his best and only the

61

sympathetic looks he received from Principal Deecke encouraged him to continue.

"Now see if you can answer one simple question about Homer satisfactorily. How did Homer describe the beaching of ships?" He drew a blank, for Albert had no idea on the subject. The examiner turned to the other boys but found they knew little more.

"This is the most ignorant class I have ever had presented to me for examination. How can you call yourselves cultured, if this is not a part of your education?"

There were a few moments of reprieve when the examiner turned the class over to a master for examination in mathematics, one subject about which he himself admitted he knew nothing. History was yet to come and while Albert ordinarily would have had no fear for his historical preparation, this was different—before this Commissioner of Education he was unsure about everything he had ever learned.

But the boy had not reckoned with the fact that history was the examiner's specialty. To his surprise, the man's anger was forgotten as he warmed to his subject and to the intelligent answers he received from Albert. Before long the student and educator were earnestly discussing the differences in the methods used by the Greeks and the Romans in establishing colonies.

When the examination was over and the commissioner announced the results, he expressed his pleasure in finding a young man with whom he could really converse on history, a young man who not only knew his historical facts but who was also capable of making good historical judgments. He had forgotten all about his remarks at the beginning of the examination and wrote "excellent" for history on Albert's certificate.

CHAPTER 5

University Study and His Life Plan

FOLLOWING a wonderful summer spent at Günsbach with his family, taking long walks over the hills, having lengthy discussions with his father and playing for many hours on the church organ, Albert left to start the next stage in his education. In October of 1893, he became a student at the University of Strasbourg and took up residence in the theological college of St. Thomas. The University was at the height of its fame. The professors were young and the students possessed all the eagerness of youth which gives such zest and meaning to education.

Albert undertook two subjects, theology, which is the study of religion, and philosophy, which is the study of the nature of wisdom and knowledge—and of course his beloved music. One of the first hurdles he had to pass was an examination in Hebrew. Although he had learned a little of the language at the Gymnasium, he had to study very hard to reach a satisfactory standing. Later on, the

64

need to be able to read Hebrew freely and the challenge that its difficulty presented led him to become a master of the subject. But meanwhile his first term at the University was somewhat spoiled by his having to devote so many hours to this language, when there was so much else that he wanted to learn. Yet he did not neglect his philosophy and theology.

Albert had to win a scholarship which would pay for his education, otherwise he could not continue. As a rule, three subjects needed to be passed for a student to obtain a scholarship, but because some of the students had to serve their period of compulsory military training, such students, which included Albert, were allowed to select one subject in place of three. Albert decided to be tested on the Gospels, and when he went away on army maneuvers he carried a Greek Testament in his pocket and spent hours each night studying the Gospels in the language in which they were originally written. During this period of his life he never felt tired, no matter what he did, and the time and thought he was able to give to this study under these unusual circumstances opened the way to his future years of research in religion, and to new ideas concerning Jesus and his teachings, no matter how busy he was.

Schweitzer was nervous about the examination, since the conclusions he had come to with regard to the nature of Jesus were not those held by his professor, so he was relieved when that sympathetic man, knowing that his student had been doing military service, only asked him to compare the contents of the first three Gospels, Matthew, Mark and Luke, which he could do easily and without embarrassment. Twenty minutes after the examination was over, Schweitzer's scholarship was awarded and his education was secure.

Albert had plenty of opportunity for reading, for research and for plain hard thinking, for the German universities do not require students to attend as many different classes as do the universities in North America, nor are the students constantly required to write examinations. Instead, they are left free to explore books and to develop their minds in their own way. That Albert Schweitzer was given such freedom is in no small measure responsible for the fact that he has been able to work out a code of living which has had so universal an appeal to mankind everywhere. He also gained certain religious convictions which were to have great influence upon the course of his life.

At the university, he was active in student associations and especially in one which gave him the opportunity to do social work. Each member of this group had to visit a certain number of poor families every week, to discover what their situations were, to give help when needed and later to report on the conditions. To get money for this project, the student also had to call on wealthy families, describe the work he was doing and ask for financial help. Since Albert was shy, he found the latter a great ordeal, but the experience taught him many valuable lessons for the time when he would be working in Africa. He discovered how important it was to ask for money with tact and—

66

Albert Schweitzer

Doctor and Mrs. Schweitzer in Oslo, after Nobel Prize ceremony, look down on youth parade

Berit Bjornstad Photo

Student torch bearers, in Oslo, Norway

A quiet moment in Lambarene

equally important—to accept it gracefully. And seeing the suffering of the poor brought his mind again and again to the thing which had troubled him since childhood. Had he a right to all his happiness and health when others were denied them? Before long he found his answer.

During a short vacation at Günsbach in early summer Albert woke one morning early to find the birds singing and the sun shining brilliantly through the trees, and there, while everything seemed wonderful, he settled the matter once and for all. Before he got up he had decided, calmly and deliberately, that he would feel himself justified in living until he was thirty, absorbing art and science and all the things of the mind that he loved, in order to devote himself from that time forward to the direct service of humanity. As a result of his decision, he discovered that his happiness had increased, that he now had an inward serenity as well as outward enjoyment of living. When he returned to the university, he found that he had an even greater capacity for work than he had had before.

Music took more and more of a hold on him, although the organ practice was in addition to his regular studies. During his early days at the university he became very familiar with the music of Bach. Ernst Münch, the brother of his music teacher in Mülhausen, was organist at St. Wilhelm's church and a specialist in Bach, and it wasn't long before Albert was playing the accompaniments during the practice sessions for the Bach concerts. Later he played in the concerts themselves, whenever the great Münch was unable to be present. This experience in playing Bach's contatas and passion music was the beginning of Albert Schweitzer's specialization in Bach's music for which he became famous. In later years he was to write books on the interpretation of Bach, as well as to become the outstanding concert artist in the playing of Bach's organ music.

Albert also loved the stirring music of Richard Wagner. He first heard Wagner's *Tannhaüser* when he was sixteen and still a student at the Gymnasium, and he was so overcome by it that days passed before he came down to earth sufficiently to do his lessons. Living in Strasbourg, he had more opportunities to hear Wagner's music played, and once he was given tickets to hear *Parsifal* at Bayreuth. After paying for the train journey, he had to live on one meal a day during all the time of his visit, but he saw and heard Wagner's opera performed and played to perfection and he never forgot the experience.

His four years as an undergraduate at the university passed all too quickly and in the summer of 1897 Albert completed his thesis which would decide whether or not he would be allowed to write the examination in theology. The thesis had a long and impressive title but it was really a study of the life of Jesus and the significance of the Last Supper. This paper was found to be satisfactory and so in the spring of 1898 Albert Schweitzer passed the first of his examinations in religion. He then turned his attention to philosophy.

He moved to a house on Old Fish Market Street, the same house in which Goethe had lived during his student days at Strasbourg. This was Albert's first real association with Goethe and it added another thread to the loom which was weaving his life into a specific design. Already he had his music, Bach in particular; his theology, which one day was to make him a minister; his philosophy, leading him to formulate his reverence for life which would have such a wide appeal; and now he had Goethe, the man who stood high as a poet, philosopher and statesman, whose work one day would take Schweitzer to America.

When his examinations were over, Albert applied for a scholarship to enable him to go on to more advanced studies. He received the Gall Scholarship which allowed him just enough to live on each year for six years. At the end of this time he must take his degree in theology at Strasbourg or else repay the money.

He had already made up his mind that, first of all, he would obtain his degree of Doctor of Philosophy and that he would take as his main subject the Religious Philosophy of Kant. And so in October of 1898 he went to Paris, to the University of the Sorbonne, to study Kant's works and to take music lessons from the famous musician Widor whom he had met through his aunt.

The Sorbonne disappointed him, however. He found the methods of instruction very antiquated and soon gave up attending lectures altogether. Furthermore, the library regulations were so rigid and complicated that studying the literature about Kant was almost impossible. Albert decided therefore to turn to Kant's own original writings

69

in German, which was a tremendous undertaking but one which gave him great satisfaction, for, whenever possible, it is always better to study directly and at firsthand rather than what other people have said or written about your subject.

Albert loved Paris immediately and felt at home there at once, like almost everyone else who has ever visited that enchanting city. Two of his uncles and their families lived in Paris and they were all good to him. Through them, he met a great many members of the university staff and before long he had a busy social life. Yet he did not allow either his thesis or his music to suffer and, since he was able to work throughout the night without any ill effect, he managed to do justice to all that he undertook.

Widor gave him organ lessons without charging for them. Pianist Philipp gave him piano lessons and from Marie Jaëll-Trautmann, whose "guinea-pig" he became, he received a completely new idea of touch in piano playing. She tried out all of her experiments on Albert and taught him how to become master of his fingers. From Philipp he received the traditional instruction and from Jaëll-Trautmann the most modern technique of the age, while he kept each of these instructors in ignorance of the fact that he was being taught by the other. It certainly saved him from becoming too one-sided, for in the morning he played in the style of Marie Jaëll-Trautmann for the satisfaction of his touch instructor and in the afternoon after the fashion of M. Philipp, for the benefit of that gentleman.

In March of 1898 the thesis on Kant was finished and Albert returned to Strasbourg where he had to read it aloud to his professor. The thesis was approved as satisfactory, although in the general oral examination which followed, he fell far short of his professor's expectations, for he had become so deeply interested in his research into the original work of Kant that he had neglected most of the textbooks about him. However, the hurdle was passed, he obtained the degree of Doctor of Philosophy, and his thesis was published in 1899.

Yet he felt the need to read more philosophy and spent the summer of that year in Berlin, reading the works of ancient and modern writers who had lived their lives in search for wisdom and knowledge.

Berlin was at the height of its glory. The intellectual life centered about its university. Society was simple and informal and Albert was invited into many homes. He was disappointed, however, in the musical style of the organists in the city and was dismayed at the tone of the new organs after playing the lovely instruments in Paris and Alsace.

On his return to Strasbourg, although he was no longer a student, he was permitted to be a paying guest at St. Thomas and to live in his old room which looked out on a quiet garden shaded by large trees. He had spent so many happy days in this room that it seemed an ideal place to continue his work. Moreover, the board and lodging were very cheap.

Albert had a feeling of obligation that he should get

71

his degree in theology as soon as possible and so release his scholarship for another needy student. He therefore started at once to prepare for the two necessary examinations. After the first of them had been passed, he obtained the post of preacher at St. Nicholas, in Strasbourg, the same church in which his Uncle Albert, for whom he was named had preached years before. Following his second examination, he became a curate. Once again his thesis on the meaning of the Last Supper was highly praised, and once again he barely passed the rest of the examination in theology because he had not studied the things in which he had not been particularly interested. The board of examiners reproached him for not knowing enough about the names and lives of the writers of the hymns, and at one point Albert excused himself by saying, "I regarded that hymn so unimportant I did not notice who wrote it," only to discover it had been written by the great poet Spitta, whose son, representing the Theology Faculty, was among the examiners.

Preaching ran in Albert Schweitzer's blood and indeed he felt it was essential to his being. He loved nothing better than standing before a congregation and discussing a religious problem. At St. Nicholas he was perfectly suited to his position. He was assistant to two elderly ministers and it fell to him to take care of the Sunday afternoon services, the children's service and the confirmation class, and nothing could have given him more joy than carrying out these duties. Albert looked upon his own talks in the services as mere devotions and often made them very short. So much so, in fact, that somebody complained and he was summoned to the rector's office. The old minister was quite as embarrassed as the younger one. Albert told him that he always stopped talking when he had no more to say, but was told by the kind old man that he should never preach for less than twenty minutes, no matter what.

As time passed, it fell to Albert to preach more often on Sunday morning as well, and these sermons he prepared with the utmost care. Occasionally he had a Sunday free, when he went to his home at Günsbach and conducted the service in the church of his childhood, taking the place of his father.

A confirmation class in Alsace continued for two years and Albert found great joy in meeting with the young people three times a week for such a period. Recalling his own experience, however, he saw to it that every boy had a chance to ask any questions that occurred to him during the instruction. He did his best to teach respect for the traditional thinking of the Church but at the same time to remember that Paul the Apostle said that wherever there is the spirit of Christ there is liberty. Most of all he wanted to put meaning into religion so that they would not turn away from it later on in life.

During the school holidays, a month at Easter and two months at the end of the summer, there were no classes and the senior pastors made it possible for their young assistant to get away. Albert therefore was able to spend the Easter weeks at Paris, visiting his uncle and aunt and continuing his organ lessons with Widor. The autumn holiday he spent in Günsbach with his family and friends. Here he found delight in walking along his beloved woodland paths.

These were quiet but important years, for during them Albert Schweitzer was able to lay the foundation for all his future creative expression—for his music, and his philosophical thinking and writing. He worked long hours and required little sleep, getting his relaxation from change of activity. He developed his powers of concentration during the hours that were full and yet unhurried. There was not enough money for traveling, although whenever he could manage it, he journeyed to Bayreuth to hear Siegfried Wagner, the son of the great Richard Wagner, give his concerts.

Apart from these occasional visits, most of Albert's free time was spent on research into the personality of Jesus as recorded in the Gospels. He was already becoming looked upon as a leading preacher. As a result of his abilities, he filled in as Principal of the Theology College from May to September of the year 1901, until the new permanent principal was able to assume his duties.

Albert Schweitzer gave his inaugural lecture before the Faculty of Theology in the following year. He was aware that there had been some opposition to his appointment and that two men in particular had disapproved of his methods of doing historical research into the lives of Jesus and Paul and feared that Dr. Schweitzer would not be a good influence upon the young men who were studying religion. They thought he would confuse them in their beliefs, but he had friends enough to override their opposition. Dr. Albert Schweitzer was now making his influence felt throughout the university and when once again a vacancy occurred, he was appointed to the permanent position of Principal of the Faculty of Theology, and in October of 1903 he moved into the beautiful official residence of the university which overlooked the river. Around it was a sunny closed-in garden, with tall trees, and here he used to walk and think and plan. The quiet, lovely solitude became part of the man himself. At the same time and in spite of his new honor, for the position he now held was the highest he could obtain as a minister and teacher, he continued to use as his study the same old room he had occupied as a student.

In this same study he worked on a review of all the literature written about Jesus all through the ages, and the number of books was so large that he had great difficulty in organizing his material and finally heaped the volumes in piles all over the study floor, where they stayed until he finished with one pile and could clear it away and start on another. For months at a time he had to protect them from the cleaning woman who wished to move them about in order to sweep the floor, and from visitors who had to step over and around the piles to hunt a chair. The result of all this, however, appeared in 1906, in his book called, Quest of the Historical Jesus.

The Sermon on the Mount influenced him profoundly, for he felt that its teaching that love, mercy and justice

75

are the heart of religion was the true basis of all liberal Christianity. Albert Schweitzer became determined to put sincerity and intellectual honesty in the search for the historic truth and the meaning of life above all else.

CHAPTER 6

Organ Music and Organ Building

For a good many years Albert Schweitzer returned to Paris during the spring and sometimes in the autumn as well, in order to continue his instruction from Widor on the organ in the church of St. Sulpice. This great teacher was especially interested in John Sebastian Bach, and the two men spent long periods together, discussing his music, its meaning and interpretation. Widor often asked Schweitzer why he didn't put down on paper just what they were talking about, for there were no books in French about Bach's music but only about his life. At last Schweitzer agreed and promised to write an essay in French for Widor's students at the Paris Conservatoire.

The idea appealed to him particularly because ever since he was eight years old, struggling to touch the pedals of the organ in Günsbach, he had not only played Bach but had thought deeply about the meaning of the music and had come to the conclusion that Bach was a painter of sound.

He set to work at once but at the end of the vacation, when his essay was supposed to be presented, he realized that he was actually writing a book, for he was completely carried away by his subject. Although French was his second language, after his native German, this was his first big attempt to express himself in it. The language seemed to hem him in, for French is a carefully refined and finished language compared with the rough and ready German. Yet as he strove for simplicity and rhythm in his writing, he at last found a style which suited him.

Research reading and writing had to be fitted into spare moments of a very busy life, and when these came late at night it was difficult to use the library. He learned by chance that a certain lady in Paris had become tired of looking at a long row of gray books which contained the complete works of Bach and would sell them for a fraction of their real value. Albert Schweitzer bought them and could then work all night long if he felt inclined. In 1905 his French book, *Bach, the Musician-Poet,* was published and dedicated to his aunt in Paris. She had first arranged for his meeting with Widor, his teacher who had taken him so far along the path of music.

In this book Schweitzer presented Bach as a poet and a painter of sound, a master who spoke in a clear language of music. If the theme concerned winds or waves or falling leaves, the music of Bach brought them vividly to the mind. The book met with enthusiasm, not only in France but in Germany too, and the author was asked to make a German translation.

A year later, when his *Quest for the Historical Jesus* was finished, Albert set to work on the German edition of the Bach book but soon found that it was impossible for him to translate from the one language to the other. He realized that it would be far better to forget what he had written in French and to start afresh on a book in which his thoughts as well as his writing would be in German from the very beginning. Even then, it was not easy and he started to write time and time again, only to put it aside. At last one night, after attending a superb performance of *Tristan* at Bayreuth, he returned to his room at the Black Horse Inn and with the voices rising from the beer garden below his window he began to write.

The small room became stuffy, the night very quiet, but his pen raced on and on, stopping only after sunrise the next morning. The German book on Bach was off to a fine start and for the next two years Schweitzer found it a joy to work on during such free time as he had. How he managed to find the time is almost a miracle for his life was seemingly fully occupied by the preparation and presentation of lectures on religion to university students, writing his Sunday sermons, and his organ concerts. He even kept up his old interest in the construction of organs. He saw the inner workings of most of the old organs within miles of any place where he lived or visited and would go far out of his way to play one whenever possible. Once when he made a special trip to Stuttgart, to see and hear a new organ which had just been installed, he was horrified to encounter harsh sounds all run together in which it was impossible to distinguish the notes at all. He realized that the tendency to junk the fine old organs simply because they were old and to replace them with new factory-built organs was a step downward. From then on, he began a one-man crusade to stop the process and as part of his effort wrote a book called *The Art of Organ Building and Organ Playing in Germany and France.*

He pointed out that the old organs were the result of generations of experimenting with the best materials and with the shapes of the pipes, and that the new kinds made by the factories had pipes that were too narrow, with walls much too thin, so that resonance was lost. He attacked the new idea that an organ could be placed anywhere in a church, wherever there happened to be room. In some churches the organ was even placed on the floor, whereas the best sound came from those which were hung high and free so that the music could flow evenly through the entire church.

With the publication of the book he became Albert Schweitzer the expert on organ-building, and he had to spend hours and hours working over designs sent to him for approval by churches all over Europe. He wrote letters by the hundred, trying to get church committees who were considering buying new factory organs to put their money into good materials instead of extra organ stops. He wrote letters and went on journeys to distant towns to try to save a condemned organ from destruction. This went on for years and years, even after he had spent much time in Africa and many of his friends began to say,

80

"In Africa Albert Schweitzer saves old Negroes, in Europe he saves old organs!" The crusade continues in fact right to this day, for he feels that in a way the struggle is in reality a struggle for truth, that the old organs sing music truthfully while the new ones confuse it and cheat the listener.

Albert Schweitzer at the age of thirty was already the principal of a college, a famous preacher, a teacher and philosopher, the greatest living authority on the music of Bach, and the organ-building expert of Europe. His life was full to overflowing with useful and creative work. His influence spread far and wide and any other man would probably have felt completely satisfied and been content to continue in such a way for the rest of his life, feeling that he was doing all that one man could do and that most of his work was in the service of man. For Albert Schweitzer, however, it was not enough, for he knew he was pleasing himself even more than he might be pleasing others. He knew that his great strength and powers must be used in another way if he was to live a life with which he would be fully content.

CHAPTER 7

Student of Medicine

THE decision Albert made that quiet sunny day years
before, as he lay in bed in Günsbach, listening to the fresh
joyous sounds of an early summer morning, never really
left his mind, for he had then decided once and for all
that when he was thirty, he would thereafter devote his
life to the service of mankind. Now the time had arrived
to make good his promise. His determination was unchanged but the kind of service he would give was still
uncertain. First, he thought of taking abandoned or
neglected children and giving them shelter, love and education, and when he moved into his spacious and sunny
theological residence he felt he had the right place for
such a home. This plan proved to be impractical.

Next the plans for service took the form of caring for
tramps, homeless persons and discharged prisoners. He
undertook to help in just such a scheme that had already
been started, expecting to enlarge and develop it if it was
enough of a challenge. Every tramp had to be looked up
and investigated before assistance was given. Day after

day Albert rode his bicycle for miles, trying to verify the truth of the stories the applicants had given him, only to find that these men were not known at the addresses indicated. Schweitzer soon realized that only an organization could manage a program of this sort and what he wanted was an independent activity in which he could act as an individual.

One evening Albert entered his study and found on the top of his writing table a green-covered magazine put out by the Paris Missionary Society. Once a month the magazine reported the activities of the missionaries in their Congo mission in Africa. It was the same journal that his father had used as a basis for his Sunday afternoon sermons in Günsbach and Albert had been interested in looking at it ever since he was a small boy. His writing lay ready for him to continue but before he sat down to write, he leafed through the magazine, and in so doing his attention was caught by an article called, *The Needs of the Congo Mission*. He read it through. The writer hoped that someone would offer to go to the Congo Colony where workers were urgently needed. Albert Schweitzer finished his reading, closed the magazine and knew his search was ended. So far, he had lived for himself. Henceforth, he would live for others and it was to Africa that he would go. And like the apostle Paul, whose writings he had studied so much, he "conferred not with flesh and blood" but laid his plans alone and without consulting anyone.

The night of October 12, 1905, Albert Schweitzer spent

in Paris writing letters. They were not easy to write and he had put the task off as long as possible. One letter was written to his parents and others to his close friends, telling them that he had decided to enter medical college, to prepare himself for work as a doctor in Equatorial Africa. Another was a letter of resignation as principal of the Theological College of St. Thomas because he could not combine his duties as principal with his study of medicine. He was putting his established career behind him and was starting afresh in a new direction, one of the hardest things a man can do.

He was not prepared, however, for the reactions of his relatives and friends who were hurt that he had not discussed or shared his plans with them. They accused him of burying his talent. They said that helping savages should be left to people without gifts such as he possessed. His music master, Widor, tried to get him to give the whole idea up. He argued that Schweitzer was already famous, that he was a well-known preacher as well as a philosopher and soon all the world would know him as a musician. Other people, plenty of them, could do such work as was needed in Africa and it would be far better to go on with the life he had been leading and in which he had already reached such heights. Others said he could do more to help the natives by giving lectures than he could in any other way. No one, in fact, could understand that a man could be swept into a new life of service simply by the love that Jesus had preached. They all looked for some hidden reason such as a disappointing

love affair or dissatisfaction with his job as preacher and teacher. Nearly everyone tried to probe into his inner person and he found it actually a relief when he met an individual who obviously thought he was crazy.

The part of his plan which seemed the strangest to his family and friends was that at the age of thirty, when he had reached such an influential position in the church,

85

he should choose to go to Africa as a medical doctor and not as a missionary. Why at the age of thirty he should become a medical student, with years of preparation ahead, seemed impossible to understand. As a matter of fact, Albert himself by no means looked forward to those years of further study, but he felt they were necessary if he was to attain what he most desired. He felt strongly that the long years as a preacher which had given him so much joy had been spent talking about the religion of love. Now he wanted to put it into practice. All the reports in the missionary magazine spoke of the physical suffering of the natives and he planned one day to ease that suffering as best he could.

He might have thought more seriously of going to Africa as a church missionary if he had felt he would have been acceptable, but he knew that it was most unlikely. He realized that his writings and sermons about Jesus as a historical person and his views concerning the nature of the Gospels made him a liberal Christian, whereas the missions were under the control of rigidly traditional Christian missionaries. Not even a man of the standing of Albert Schweitzer could serve as a missionary when his personal interpretations differed so essentially with the principles on which the mission was founded.

Schweitzer was familiar with the Paris Society which ran the Congo mission and was not at all surprised when the mission director, who was very pleased to find that his appeal for help had been read, told him that there were serious objections to his religious views which would

have to be cleared away before his offer of service could
be considered. When Schweitzer told him that he wanted
to go only as a medical doctor and not as a missionary,
the director was greatly relieved. Soon, however, he wrote
to Schweitzer saying that some of the Society members
objected to his going into the field as a mission doctor.
However, since several years would be required for his
medical training, Albert decided not to force the issue
at that time but hoped that a way would open up later on.

Yet he clung to his original desire to serve in the Paris
mission in Equatorial Africa. Partly it was because he had
first responded to the appeal in the magazine, partly because the mission stories he heard as a child had affected
him so much, and perhaps even more because deep inside
him lay the memory of the statue of the sad-eyed Negro
in Colmar. His heart had responded to the tragic appeal
of that African face, just as it had to the gentle smile of
the old persecuted Jew.

Can you imagine what it was like to have been the
principal of one of the colleges in a great university
and to resign such a post to become a student again at
the age of thirty in the same university? No wonder the
Dean of the Medical School thought the eminent Doctor
Albert Schweitzer must be out of his mind when he regis-
tered for the first year medical course. It created a situation that was entirely new. Dr. Schweitzer would
continue to be a professor in the theology college, for he
had resigned only as principal; yet as a professor, he could
not register as a student but was entitled to visit any

class he wished. As a class visitor, however, he was not qualified to take examinations, and unless he wrote his examinations he could not receive his degree. The problem was solved by having all the professors sign a paper saying that Albert Schweitzer had attended the lectures and should be allowed to sit for the examinations, and since the student in this case was a professor like themselves, the governing body decided not to require any fees.

So less than a month after he had sent in his letter of resignation as Principal of the Theology College, Albert attended his first lecture as a medical student, the beginning of a course of studies that were to continue for seven years. And for the first time in his life he had to fight incessant fatigue. He had kept his position as a lecturing professor because he needed the salary, but it involved a great deal of work. In addition, he continued his research on the teachings of Paul and was anxious to write it into a book as a companion to his *Quest for the Historical Jesus*. His duties as Principal of the College continued for several months after he had started his medical studies, and even after they came to an end, he found he could not bring himself to give up his preaching at St. Nicholas, for it brought him both satisfaction and money which he needed. His organ playing also demanded time, for he was becoming well known and was in frequent demand for concerts. He loved his music, of course, and the concert money made up for what he lost when he ceased to be Principal of the Theological School. Many trips were made to Paris to play the organ in the Bach Society Concerts, attending only the final practice and the performance itself and then sitting up all night on the train in order to prepare a sermon or a lecture. For some concerts, Schweitzer even went as far as Barcelona in Spain. He had insufficient time to do all that he wished, and only just enough strength to carry on these activities. And throughout these long years of medical training, he was continually tired almost to the point of dropping.

Albert Schweitzer dreaded leaving the principal's residence for he had lived there ever since he was a student. He loved the garden and the tall trees and felt he could not part with them. Once again good fortune stepped in and he was given four small attic rooms, high up under the gables, but still part of St. Thomas's and so enabling him to go on using the garden. There was no necessity to tear himself up by the roots but only to carry his things out of one door and upstairs to his new home. The move took place on a rainy Shrove Tuesday, 1906, and the theology students being free came to help him. Moreover, since the new principal and his family made him welcome, he was able to go in and out of his old place as freely as he wished.

A distinguished noblewoman, Countess Louisa of Erlach, was an aged and almost helpless member of the household, quite unable to go out to attend concerts. Yet she loved music and so every evening Albert spent one precious hour out of his all-too-short day, playing the piano for her, knowing the joy that it brought.

I wish it were possible to say that Schweitzer's medical studies came easily, but they did not. When a man is over

89

thirty, it is much more difficult to memorize whole new fields of knowledge than it is at twenty. In addition, as with his earlier studies, Albert became carried away by what interested him most, which was pure science, and he would not listen to the youths who insisted that he must prepare to pass the examinations. His fellow students had been cramming for a long time and it was only a few weeks before the examinations that he made himself join them. However, he passed with good marks, although his fatigue was almost unbearable.

The second term as a medical student was a little easier for Albert because the subjects were more closely related, while his ever present need for funds was relieved by the sales of his German book on Bach and by the many concerts he was able to give. He even managed to earn the fee required for his state medical examination by playing the organ part of a new musical work composed and conducted by his friend and teacher, Widor.

At long last, a week before Christmas, 1911, Albert Schweitzer walked out of the building where his final examination in medicine had been held and looked up at the stars in the black, cold, cloudless sky. It seemed like a dream and he could hardly believe that he had reached his goal. Only his excellent health had made it possible for him to continue with his theology, music, research and writing while he studied medicine. All that was left now was a year of internship in a hospital and a presentation of a thesis. Then his African adventure could begin. Yet during that year Albert succeeded in getting his book on St. Paul ready for publication and also the first five volumes of Bach's organ music, with directions on how it should be played.

He shared this study of Bach with Widor and they worked together in Paris or in the quiet village of Güns-bach, where there could be no interruptions. John Sebastian Bach had left very few instructions concerning how his music ought to be played because when he wrote it, none were necessary. The old organs could not be played either as fast or as loud as the new ones and an organist naturally played the music the way it was written. When the new organs came in, Bach's music was more or less murdered, and after Widor and Schweitzer had worked out how it should be treated, they felt it important to share their knowledge with other lovers of Bach. They managed to finish only the sonatas, concertos, preludes and fugues before the time came for Schweitzer's departure for Africa, but the work was published in French, German and English.

For his medical thesis, Albert decided to write a psychiatric study of Jesus, for by doing so he could combine his medical knowledge with his research on Jesus as a historical person. At the same time, he had other things to do, for he had sadly to bring an end to the university teaching and the preaching at St. Nicholas that he had done for so long and had loved so much. His last sermon finished with the words, "The Peace of God which passeth all understanding, keep your heart and mind in Christ Jesus." It was the way in which he had ended his sermons throughout the years but now the words took on a deeper meaning. No one knew how it hurt him to close a door on this part of his life. From that day until he actually left he avoided the street where his beloved St. Nicholas stood and also the university buildings, for the pain of knowing he had finally cut the strings to his old life and would never pick them up again was too great to bear.

In other ways, however, his life was just beginning. He turned his mind to the thought of marriage to Helene, daughter of Professor Bresslau who was the director of historical studies at Strasbourg University.. He had first known her as a student and she had assisted him in all his plans and had been a constant help with his work, spending long hours checking his manuscripts and correcting proofs. She understood his reason for undertaking the African service and shared his enthusiasm. She gave up her own work and trained as a nurse so that she could help him in the best way possible, and in June of 1912 they were married.

Earlier in the year, while he was in Paris taking a special course in Tropical Medicine, Albert had begun to order the equipment he needed to start a hospital in Africa. Together the Schweitzer couple now made lists of the housekeeping goods they would need for living in the primeval forest. Everything had to be especially ordered.

How did Albert Schweitzer finance such an adventure? He begged! He called on everyone he knew for financial help. He had nothing to show, merely an idea and his own personality. His friends contributed generously; the professors in Strasbourg gave liberally; his congregation, his past students joined in; and money came also from the Paris Bach Society. Finally, Albert had enough to buy the necessary things to outfit a small hospital completely. Only then did he once again visit the Paris Missionary Society to offer his services.

Dr. Schweitzer offered to go at his own expense to the mission field at Lambaréné, on the River Ogowe in French Equatorial Africa, to serve as medical doctor to the natives. The director of the society thought the offer should be accepted but some members of the committee objected. So the doctor was asked to appear before the committee for questioning concerning his beliefs. He said he could not come before the committee as such but that he would gladly call upon each member of the committee separately to talk with them and let each see for himself whether he, Albert Schweitzer, would be of service to the Negro natives and a credit to the society.

Several afternoons were given to making these calls and some of the members confessed that their hesitation was caused by the fear that Schweitzer's beliefs and learnings might confuse the missionaries in Africa, and that they also were afraid that he wanted to preach to the natives as well as give them medical aid. Most of the committee members, when they were assured that he wished to serve only in a medical capacity, became quite friendly. The committee finally accepted Dr. Schweitzer's offer of free medical service.

One more hurdle remained and the road would be clear His medical diploma was from a German university and he had to get permission from the French Colonial Department to practice in a French possession. Influential friends in Paris helped him obtain the necessary papers, and Dr. and Mrs. Albert Schweitzer could leave for Africa!

Seventy packing cases were shipped to the port of Bordeaux, on the west coast of France, in February, 1913, shortly after Albert's thirty-eighth birthday. In one of them was a piano, specially built to withstand the heat and damp of the tropics and fitted with organ pedal attachments. This was a gift of the Paris Bach Society in appreciation of the years he had served as its organist. Now only four weeks remained in which to visit close friends and relatives.

At last there was just the hand baggage to pack. When Mrs. Schweitzer saw that her husband was taking along 2000 marks in gold she questioned the wisdom of it. But Albert Schweitzer had already heard enough concerning the political unrest in Europe to know that war was possible, and he knew that, if war did break out, only gold coinage would be of any value.

CHAPTER 8

The African Adventure

THE train pulled into the station at Günsbach on Good Friday, 1913, just as the church bells ceased ringing for the afternoon service. Dr. Schweitzer and his wife once again said their farewells to the Schweitzer family and friends and climbed aboard the last coach. They waved good-bye as long as they could see the church steeple. Their adventure had started and they were very excited, although the memory of the bells and the last view of the church above the tree tops would always linger in their minds.

The following day the couple said good-bye to their friends in Strasbourg, and again they watched the cathedral as the train drew away from the town. The morning of Easter Sunday, they sat in St. Sulpice Church in Paris and listened to the old organ being played by Widor. By two o'clock they were aboard the train for Bordeaux, traveling through the countryside of France. The day was gloriously bright. Spring was in the air, the village folk were in their holiday dress, and above the noise of the train they could hear the sound of the village church bells as they sped along.

On Easter Monday, they arrived at the Bordeaux customs house to get their luggage, which had been sent on ahead, only to find it closed for the day. After a frantic search, they finally found an official who was able to let them get their cases. With two cars filled to the brim, they rushed to the harbor station, where the boat train was just about to leave, taking the passengers to the ship *Europe,* on which the Schweitzers were to sail for Africa.

Exhausted, Albert and his wife sank into their seats on the train and for more than an hour sat watching the cloudless blue sky and the green and yellow and brown fields. It was long enough for them to regain strength to push their way among the boxes and barrels and reach the narrow gangplank which led onto the boat itself. At last they found themselves in a large cabin, placed well forward from the ship's engines, and they were well pleased, for it would be their home for the next three weeks. They had just sufficient time to wash before the bell rang for dinner and they went to the ship's dining room to eat and to meet their fellow passengers.

Most of the other travelers were returning to Africa after a rest in Europe and they were able to tell the Schweitzers much about their future home. There was little opportunity to make friends, however, for the second day at sea the Bay of Biscay lived up to its reputation and a storm blew up, tossing the good ship *Europe* and its unhappy passengers this way and that for three whole days.

Dr. Schweitzer was an inexperienced traveler and had not securely fastened the trunks to the cabin walls with rope. He and his young wife awoke during the first night of the storm to find every movable object crashing from one side of the cabin to the other. Albert sprang out of bed, intending to make them fast, but nearly had a leg crushed between a trunk and the wall. The rest of the night he spent counting the seconds between the plunge of the ship and the crash of the boxes, listening also to the sound of dishes smashing on the floor of the dining room and ship's galley. In the morning a friendly steward showed the Doctor how to tie the baggage securely so that it no longer dashed about the floor. Those passengers who tried to stand and walk around had many accidents and injuries, while the ship's cook could not go near the stove so that all food had to be served cold.

After three days of discomfort the storm subsided and the sea quieted and life aboard ship became normal once more.

Most of the passengers were army officers or traders. One of them, an army doctor who had served for twelve years in Equatorial Africa, agreed to spend two hours each morning with Dr. Schweitzer and give him valuable lessons concerning the Negroes he was going to help and about the diseases he was most likely to encounter.

On the fourth day out, when the air was cool and fresh, no warmer than a day in June, the army officers all put on their sun helmets. Dr. and Mrs. Schweitzer found this queer, but, as they stood at the rail of the ship, watching their first sunset at sea, a seasoned African came up to them and said, "Starting tomorrow, you must think of the sun as your worst enemy, and although you do not feel the heat, you must wear your sun helmets, even if it is early or at sunset or cloudy. Never expose your head to the sky, for you can get sunstroke much easier than you know." They quickly carried out his suggestion, and were to learn that this was valuable information to have and heed, although the danger was less than was thought.

The ship arrived at Dakar at last and the passengers all went ashore. The Schweitzers for the first time stood on the land to which they would devote their lives. Together with their new friends they walked up the steep, narrow streets. As they slowly climbed the hill in the intense heat, avoiding the bad holes in the road, they overtook a cart piled high with wood on which sat two large Negroes, beating and screaming at their poor horse who could not move it another inch. Doctor Schweitzer was so disturbed by the cruelty that he went over and commanded the men to get down and push. In great surprise, they obeyed and the three of them pushed the cart out of the hole it had caught in. When he rejoined his wife and friends, one who knew Africa well said, "If you cannot stand to see animals mistreated, you have no business in Africa, for here we see that kind of horror all the time." But Albert Schweitzer had not really changed since he was a young boy, and indeed as the years had gone by he had become even more sensitive to the pain of animals. Now he was determined to do everything he possibly could to ease their suffering, as well as that of human beings.

Before the ship left Dakar to continue its voyage a large number of Senegalese soldiers came aboard, together with their wives and children. They occupied the whole of the foredeck, and when night came on each person crept head first into a big sack and went to sleep. The women and children, even the smallest babies, all wore charms around their necks, sewed up in small bags.

Much of the time the Schweitzers sat quietly watching the shore line slip past and rearranging their previous ideas of what Africa was like. They had imagined desert lands and now, instead, all they saw were tall trees like a dark green wall stretching down to the water's edge. In the evening the surface appeared phosphorescent and each small jellyfish became a lighted disc. Flying fish rose out of the waves and sometimes landed on the deck. And at all times the heat was intense, even worse on cloudy days than sunny. Sharks swarmed close to the boat, but in spite of this, whenever a harbor was reached, the natives dived for coins thrown into the water by the passengers. The divers made such a noise that the sharks probably were scared away, although the last diver to come up could make no sound at all, since his mouth was chock full with the coins he had gathered.

The ship passed the Pepper Coast, the Ivory Coast and the Gold Coast and the Slave Coast. At each stop, more of the Schweitzers' friends departed and they stood at the ship's rail to call, "Good health to you," words that took on very serious meaning, for the climate of Africa is hard on white people, and after a year in residence they become tired and anemic. If they remain two or three years, they find it almost impossible to do any work at all and have to return to their homes for eight months or a year to build up their strength again.

Farther along the coast, on Sunday, April 13, the ship docked at Liberville, a place which got its name from the fact that it was here that the freed or rescued slaves were sent at the time the English and French were trying to put a stop to the slave trade. The American missionary stationed here was at the dock to greet the Schweitzers. He had brought a gift of fruit and vegetables from the mission garden, as well as an invitation to come with him to visit the mission. Here they were met by cheerful, smiling Negroes, which pleased them, for they had not grown used to the sullen looks on the faces of the workers along the coast. They were relieved to see clean bamboo huts and to shake hands with happy natives. Here were natives such as had been used as the model for the giant Negro statue in the Square at Colmar. The statue had haunted Albert Schweitzer and now it seemed to have come to life.

Finally, at Cape Lopez, the Schweitzers transferred to the river boat *Alembe* which had stern paddles and was built broad and shallow so as to be able to navigate the Ogowe River. It was already so full of cargo that only passengers and their personal luggage could be taken aboard; the cases would have to travel in a couple of weeks, when the boat made the next trip.

100

The *Alembe* entered the Ogowe River and very shortly the forest and the water seemed to merge one into the other. The tall trees reflected in the still surface seemed to be part of the forest, while the water itself blended with the trees on the land. Gradually the clumps of palm trees gave way to stretches of papyrus grass, with here and there a branch or trunk of a dead tree standing starkly alone. Birds flew up whenever the boat drew near the shore, ospreys circled overhead and dove in front of the boat to catch a surfacing fish, while great herons spread their long wings and flew from shore to shore. The chattering of monkeys blended with the songs of blue birds. Yellow-colored streams joined the river, while the river itself widened to a lake around almost every bend.

Albert Schweitzer stood watching the large Negro pilot as he turned the wheel, skilfully guiding the boat along a narrow channel as the river broadened. No chart was used, or ever existed, and the pilot had successfully taken the boat for sixteen years over invisible sand bars and around floating logs. A stop was made at a Negro village to take on wood which the natives had collected for the boat to use for fuel, and over the gangplank a line of Africans walked, each one carrying a log. On the deck one Negro stood with paper and pencil in his hand. When ten men had passed, the foreman called, "put down a one." After ten "ones" had been marked he again called out, "Make a cross." So the logs were counted, and for every hundred logs, four or five francs were paid, with all of the payment being given out in the form of alcohol. A man at

101

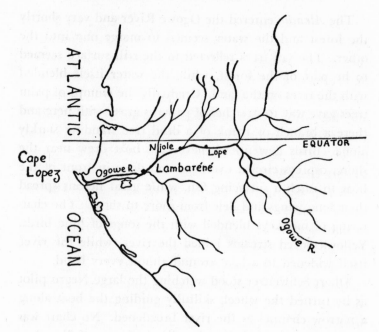

Schweitzer's side said, "The alcohol white man has brought to the Negroes of Africa is their ruin—nothing white men can do will ever make up for the damage they have done with their diseases and rum." Albert hoped earnestly that he could help remove some of the suffering caused by contact with white civilization.

There was a long way left to go. The Ogowe River itself runs seven to eight hundred miles and is navigable by river steamer for two hundred and fifty miles, as far as N'Djole; from there on, it runs between mountains and with many rapids until it reaches the Great Plateau of

Central Africa. By moonlight the shores were even blacker and more mysterious than before. Soon after midnight they reached a bad stretch of water and anchored for the night, waiting until dawn so that the pilot could avoid the snags. At five A.M. the engines were started again and the voyage continued. At N'Gomo the Schweitzers visited the mission and local sawmill, for although the land grows coffee, pepper, vanilla, cocoa and oil palms, it was the big trees that brought white men to the scene. Good timber grows there and, since the river has no sand bar where it enters the sea, heavy rafts can be floated down to waiting ships without danger of loss. Most of the West African rivers have sand bars at their mouths, which is why there are so few good harbors.

After five more hours of traveling upstream, the steamer sounded its siren for the stop at Lambaréné, a good half hour before that place came in sight so as to give the natives in their canoes time to reach the landing before the steamer arrived.

The Lambaréné mission where Dr. and Mrs. Schweitzer were going was another hour's trip by canoe and they had no expectation that anyone would meet them at the village. But as they stood watching the unloading, a long narrow canoe filled with dark skinned singing boys shot around the river boat so fast that a white man standing in the stern of the smaller craft had to sit down to avoid being hit by the cables. The mission school had come to welcome the new arrivals, racing in two canoes. Mr. Christol, one of the missionaries, in the canoe with the younger boys, won the race. Mr. Ellenburger, the other missionary, was in the losing boat. The winners were allowed to take the Schweitzers aboard, and the losers their luggage.

The canoes were merely hollowed-out tree trunks—long, flat and narrow, and the boys stood up, each wielding a long paddle which he dipped into the water to the rhythm of a song. Dr. and Mrs. Schweitzer were both nervous, for it did not seem possible that they could finish the last lap of their journey safely. The two canoes began to race with the steamer, which by now had unloaded and was moving upstream. They almost ran into another canoe, manned by three old Negroes, but, with much laughter and shouts echoing from the river boat, the accident was avoided, and by the time they had turned out of the main river into a side stream the doctor and his wife were fully relaxed and enjoying the ride.

White buildings high on a hill caught the sunlight and the Schweitzers saw the mission station for the first time. The canoe glided into a small bay where several natives, Mrs. Christol, the school mistress and the manual worker were waiting to welcome them. All of the residents conducted the newcomers to their cottage on the top of a hill. The wooden house, with a balcony all the way round it, had been decorated with palm leaves and flowers by the school children. With their new friends, the Schweitzers stood looking at the view and found it pleasing beyond words, for the river below them widened into a lake and in the distance the River Ogowe itself could be seen as a silver ribbon. The primeval forest surrounded them on three sides and while they watched, the tropical dusk came suddenly and all was dark. The children were taken to attend evening prayer and Albert and his wife stood alone, listening to the night noises of the jungle and the sound of children singing hymns. Then they knew that they had chosen rightly. This was what they had dreamed of. Now they were truly in Africa.

The day was not quite over, for there was supper with the Christols and talk of Europe and world affairs, since the missionaries were hungry for first hand news. Then the school children came to the verandah and under paper lantern decorations sang a song to a Swiss melody which Mr. Ellenburger had written and the children had learned as a special welcome to Africa for the doctor and his wife.

CHAPTER 9

The Jungle Hospital

THE Lambaréné Mission stood on three hills, lying between the river and the dense jungle. The boys' school stood on one of them, with a storehouse and mission house on the slope. On another stood the girls' school and another mission house, while in between, on the middle hill, was the house of Dr. Schweitzer. Coffee bushes, cocoa, orange, lemon, mango and pawpaw trees and oil palms covered the hill slopes, all planted by the early missionaries, for Africa is very poor in native fruit trees. The Schweitzers were very glad to find them there.

The cleared ground was only 650 yards long and about 120 yards wide, and here the doctor and his wife took their walks in the evenings and on Sundays, for the narrow paths through the jungle were so hemmed in by tall trees that no breeze could penetrate and they were stiflingly and unbearably hot. It was only when the sand banks of the river were exposed during the dry season that they could really stretch their legs and feel the cooler air from the water.

The missionaries had given out strict orders that no

serious cases were to be brought to the doctor until he had
had time to get settled. Earlier, they had expected to have
a small hospital ready for him when he arrived, but they
could not get workers to build it, since the timber trade
was too good and well paid at the time for the missionaries
to be able to induce anyone to help them. Yet the sick
arrived in spite of the fact that Dr. Schweitzer had no place
in which to examine them. He could not take them into
his own house, for fear of infection. Nor could he turn
them away, so he had to do his work out in the open,
under the hot sun mostly. When it rained, everything
had to be moved in a hurry to his verandah.

Working outdoors was very fatiguing, and at first Dr.
Schweitzer did not even have his medical supplies, since
they were in the boxes left on the Lambaréné village landing, to be delivered on the next trip made by the river
boat. Another difficulty concerned language. An interpreter had been hired but had not shown up, and slowly
the doctor came to realize that it was impossible to rely
upon the natives he had come to help.

Then one night late in April the Schweitzers heard the
river boat and rushed down to the landing to get their
much needed boxes, only to find that they had been put
ashore at the Catholic Mission at the head of the small
river as the captain was afraid to make a landing in the
dark at the mission. The boat brought two missionaries
and ten natives from the N'Gomo mission who had come
to help the doctor with his unpacking and settling in.
Without their help he would have been in trouble, for

now all the boxes, including his special piano in its zinc-lined case, must be brought by dugout canoe, and as to how this could be done he had no idea. However, a canoe was found which had been made from such a gigantic tree that it could have carried five pianos if necessary. Everyone helped, even the school children, and in three days all the boxes were safely landed and carried up the hill to the doctor's house.

It became harder and harder to examine patients in the open, with the added disadvantage of having to make a trip to the house for every bandage and bottle of medicine, but there appeared to be no chance of obtaining even a one-room hospital in the near future. In desperation, Dr. Schweitzer turned his hen house into a hospital by whitewashing the walls, putting up shelves, and setting up an old camp bed. There were no windows and it was very hot, but at least he could reach over to a shelf for his medicines whenever he needed some, and when it rained he could carry on his work without interruption.

One day he found among his patients a young man called Joseph Azdawani who seemed bright and who had a great capacity for languages; and, although he had been a cook, Albert Schweitzer asked him to remain as his interpreter and medical assistant. Joseph agreed and until he learned better it was amusing to hear him apply the only names he knew for the parts of the body, such as "This woman has a pain in her right leg of mutton." Yet Joseph was one native the doctor could rely on. He possessed a great many good qualities. Although he could neither read nor write, he had a photographic mind and never made a mistake when he reached to the shelf for medicine. He remembered the look of the label, but the letters themselves meant nothing to him. Besides this remarkable picture memory, he had the ability to speak many languages, which was a great help to the doctor. Joseph could converse in French and English and knew eight native dialects. He was alone, for his wife had left him and he had not saved enough money to buy another one. He was not even sure he wanted another wife, for while a wife could be payed for in installments, a man's life was made pretty uncomfortable by her people until she was entirely paid for. So Joseph was satisfied and proud to be the doctor's first assistant and from him the doctor learned a great deal concerning the ways in which to handle the Negro nature, although he could not always bring himself to put it into practice. Joseph, for instance, thought that the doctor should refuse to do anything for a patient he could not cure, that, just as witch doctors will do nothing to damage their reputation as healers, so a medical doctor should refrain as well. Out of this, however, came something which was a valuable lesson to have learned—never tell a patient that he can be cured or helped if the case is hopeless, but warn the patient and his family of the dangers from the very start, so that death will not be unexpected. Then if the patient lives, the white doctor and his medicine are wonderful. Albert Schweitzer discovered too that the Negro recognizes death as a natural event and is not afraid of it.

109

Joseph was quick to learn and when later N'Zeng, the interpreter originally hired, showed up, both men were found to be needed, for Joseph was a member of the Zaloa tribe and N'Zeng a member of the Pahouins, and most of the people who came to be treated came from these two tribes.

Every morning the two interpreters read the doctor's standing orders aloud to the patients, and these were the orders:

1. It is strictly forbidden to spit near the doctor's house.
2. Do not talk loudly.
3. Since the waiting may be long, all patients must bring food for the day.
4. No one may spend the night at the hospital station without permission from the doctor. If he does, he will not be given medicine.
5. Bottles and tin boxes containing medicine must be returned.
6. The doctor can see only the most urgent cases during the time the boat goes up the river and returns, for the doctor is then busy writing to Europe for more medicine.

The people nodded their heads to show that they understood and then waited patiently until their turns came. After treatment, each patient was given a round piece of cardboard on a fiber string to tie about his neck. This had a number on it corresponding to one outlining the case in the doctor's card file. On this card there was also kept a record of the medicine given out in bottles and tins, for only in this way could the doctor demand the return of the containers. The supply of bottles and boxes was always low and in the damp tropics medicine must be kept in glass or tin containers. About half the bottles and cans were saved and returned by the patients, but the tags tied about their necks they preserved carefully. To the Pahouins, they were a kind of fetish or magic charm. As there is no word for "doctor" in their language they speak of him as *Oganga,* which means fetishman. In fact, the Negroes believe that anyone who can cure pain can produce it, too. All their diseases are attributed to evil spirits and never to natural causes. When asked by a doctor to describe their symptoms, they talk of "the worm," which is what they picture pain to be, and describe how the worm was first in their legs and then moved to their heads. All medicine is taken to drive "the worm" out of their bodies.

Right from the start there were thirty to forty persons a day to be examined and treated. They suffered from skin diseases, malaria, sleeping sickness, heart disease, leprosy, dysentery, elephantiasis, and many others. One disease which caused the Negroes more pain than almost anything else was the itch. A patient would arrive at the hospital after weeks of sleepless nights from the incessant itching and with the entire body covered with infected sores from scratching. The treatment was simple, for all the patient had to do was to bathe in the river and then cover his entire body with a salve. He was given a tin of the same salve to take back to his village, with directions to repeat

the treatment twice. The treatment was always successful
and the reputation of the White Doctor spread throughout
the jungle.

The medicines soon began to run short and Dr. Schweitzer also needed a hospital building badly. Some of the
patients came two hundred and fifty miles by canoe and
brought their families, who must wait until the patient
could be taken back again. Yet they could count on finding the doctor whenever they arrived. Albert Schweitzer
was there only to serve and he could always be reached.
Every day, however, his problems became greater. He was
never sure that the patient would not eat the salve and
rub the powders into the sores, or swallow all the pills at
once. Yet the joy he saw on the faces of those who had new
clean bandages in place of rags or runny sores was enough
to make all his efforts worthwhile.

Plans had been made to build the new hospital on the
same hill as that occupied by the boys' school, but Dr.
Schweitzer soon saw that there would not be enough room
and that he needed to have the hospital at the foot of the
hill on which his own house stood. In order to make such
a change in plans, it was necessary to go with Mr. Christol
and Mr. Ellenburger to a conference of missionaries at
Samkita.

This was Dr. Schweitzer's first long trip by canoe. They
departed early one morning, about two hours before sunrise, sitting one behind the other in folding chairs in the
bow of the canoe. Their tin boxes, folding beds and mattresses, and bananas for the natives to eat, were piled in the

middle, while six pairs of paddlers occupied the stern, singing a song of their own making about where they were going, who was in the canoe, and how hard it was to paddle.

As the canoe shot out into the main river, the sun rose and, as if by command, the singing stopped abruptly. Directly in front of them were many large dark animals— hippopotami—which were bathing in the cooling water after spending the night grazing on the near-by land. The natives are afraid of these great beasts and always avoid them as far as possible, for there are many stories about how the hippos have attacked canoes and killed the occupants. At sunrise, too, the tsetse fly becomes active and, as this is the carrier of the dreaded sleeping sickness, it has to be kept off. The black insect appears to avoid settling on any light material where it can be seen and lands without any warning buzz on the dark skin of the natives, so that they are constantly fighting it.

The paddlers kept as close as possible to the shore, where the current is weakest and where the shade of the overhanging trees protects travelers from the sun. But everyone looked out for the poisonous black snakes with yellow stripes which lie along the limbs of trees, waiting to catch unwary birds and all too ready to drop into a canoe passing below. Whenever this happens, the natives jump overboard and those who cannot swim usually get drowned. Albert was more than interested when the missionaries pointed out the dangers to him as they went along.

The conference was a very satisfactory experience and Dr. Schweitzer was deeply impressed with the men he met who were devoting their lives to the welfare of the native Negroes. Here love and service were the order of the day and none of them was afraid of the ideas of Albert Schweitzer, the theologian. They needed his help as a doctor and they accepted his service in the same spirit with which they offered their own. They agreed that he should build the hospital wherever he wished and gave him eighty pounds towards the cost.

On the return journey the mission canoe had close contact with the hippos again. Several large animals swam alongside the canoe. One baby remained on the sand bar and would not obey the urging of its mother to enter the water. The incident passed without trouble, but Dr. Schweitzer was soon to treat a boy who had been so badly hurt by one of these creatures that he died in consequence.

It was after dark when the singing of the native paddlers grew louder and Dr. Schweitzer suddenly saw a line of torch lights moving down the hill at Lambaréné. The women were coming down to the landing to welcome the men home.

Eight Negroes were hired from a timber merchant to level the site of the hospital. With Dr. Schweitzer using a spade himself while the Negro foreman lay in the shade under a tree, they had the dirt cleared away in two days. As soon as the workers were paid they went directly to the store to exchange the money for alcohol! Now, however, the corrugated iron walls could be put up, and in November Dr. and Mrs. Schweitzer and Joseph moved out of the hen house into the new hospital. The new establishment had four rooms. Two of these each thirteen feet square were used as a consulting room and an operating room. Two smaller rooms at the side served as a dispensary and a sterilizing room. The floor was cement and the windows had no glass, just fine netting to keep out the flies and mosquitoes, while the ceiling was made of white cotton material, tightly stretched.

Now that there was room enough to move about, the doctor's wife helped teach Joseph how to sterilize the instruments and to prepare patients for operations. She taught him how to help her give the anesthetics and she also found time to supervise the boiling of all the used bandages, for it was necessary to use them over and over again. To her went the job of seeing that everything was clean and in order at the hospital, that the medicine bottles were filled and the instruments were ready to use. She always came on duty at ten and stayed until twelve and returned again in the afternoon, if there was an operation. To be able to be away from her household tasks at all took a great amount of managing, for in Africa the running of even such a simple house as the Schweitzers' was a full time job. Each servant did only the one thing he was hired for—the cook cooked, the laundryman washed and ironed, the boy swept the house and fed the chickens. When their jobs were over, they rested and Mrs. Schweitzer had to do all the hundred and one additional things necessary to run a home. All this was complicated by the fact that no servant could be left alone in the house, even for a moment. Besides that they needed to be watched to see

115

that they did their work, so everything had to be put under lock and key to keep it from "walking away." The natives do not take this as an insult, rather they expect the white people to protect their possessions so that their servants will not be tempted to take them or be held responsible if anything disappears. The African Negroes have the general idea that it is all right to take anything from a white person who is careless enough to leave it out. (Even Joseph insisted that the medicine cabinet be locked every time the Schweitzers left the hospital.) The value of the article does not seem to be important but the African picks up anything which attracts him at the moment. The doctor "lost" a copy of Bach's *Passion Music* on which he had spent hours writing the organ accompaniment. Mrs. Schweitzer not only had to keep all movable household articles locked up but she had to keep all food under lock and key. Each day she gave the cook exactly the amount of salt, rice, spices, etc., which were to be used. Wherever she went, she had to carry a heavy bunch of keys which could never be put down for a moment. All this was a trial to any housewife, but Mrs. Schweitzer was still able to undertake the hospital responsibilities as well.

Work was next started on two native type huts of unhewn logs and raffia leaves, one to be used for a waiting room and the other to house the patients. Both Mr. Christol and Dr. Schweitzer helped in the building of these and also a separate hut for Joseph. The dormitory hut was forty-two feet long and just under twenty feet wide and when it was finished, Dr. Schweitzer used a pointed stick

to mark sixteen rectangles in the earthen floor. These indicated sixteen beds. Then the patients and their attendants were brought in. Each patient lay on a marked out space and the attendants were given axes and told to build the beds. Within fifteen minutes they were all out in the canoes, hunting up and down the shore of the river for suitable wood and by nightfall all the beds were ready; four posts with fork ends, two long side poles, many short pieces bound crosswise and tied with creepers. They gathered dried grass for mattresses. Under the twenty-inch high beds they stored their cooking utensils, rag bundles, cooking pots, and the ever-present bananas. Always two or three people slept in one bed and the only rule was that the sick person was to be one of them, and not be forced to sleep on the floor, leaving the healthy in full possession of the bed. Families attending patients have even been known to enter the boys' dormitory, putting the boys out and sleeping in their beds. These arrangements only made Dr. Schweitzer realize that he soon must have a place for the family attendants to sleep apart, in addition to having an isolation cottage for infectious cases and a strong hut for the mentally ill.

Although there seemed to be relatively fewer mental cases in the African jungle than in Europe, their pitiful condition worried the doctor greatly. Because no bamboo hut was strong enough to restrain mentally ill persons they were brought to the hospital bound in cords. The hospital was not equipped to care for such illness, yet Dr. Schweit-

118

zer knew that to refuse would mean that the afflicted would be killed.

The doctor could not forget his first such case. It was a dark night and he found the patient tied to a palm tree. Her family sat about a fire in front of her. They protested when the doctor asked them to set her free but finally obeyed. Once free, the patient sprang at the doctor and her family ran screaming into the black forest to watch from a safe distance. They saw him seize her arm and force her to the ground. He gave the poor woman an injection in her arm which quieted her, so that after a while she followed the doctor into a hut where she soon fell asleep. In a couple of weeks she returned to her village, well for the time being, since her attack had passed. Of course, the word soon spread that the White Doctor was a magician who could even cure mad people and more and more patients suffering from mental ills were brought to the hospital. Unfortunately, many of these cases were madness which resulted from poisoning and for these there were no Western medicines which were effective.

The natives are very secretive about the poison plants they use and any man or woman who revealed the knowledge to a white person would soon be a victim of the poison himself. Medicine men used these poisons to keep their authority over the village folk. Most of the people were in constant fear of being poisoned by their enemies or of having the "evil eye" cast on them. Certain individuals were believed to possess the power or fetish to cause harm to another person. The fetish or charm was some-

119

times a red feather or a leopard's claw or a bit of human skull (the owner was killed especially for the making of the fetish). Whatever it was made of, its power completely controlled the actions of the superstitious Africans.

During his first nine months in Africa and out of his first 2000 cases, Dr. Schweitzer did not come across a single instance of cancer or appendicitis. There was always much suffering from chills and head colds and most of the old people died of pneumonia. Many complained of rheumatism and their living conditions did little to help their suffering. Bad teeth caused much pain and many begged the doctor to pull their teeth so they could have false teeth. A few old people were greatly envied because they possessed store teeth.

The doctor soon learned the value of the warning given against going out in the sun without the head covered, for the wife of one of the missionaries walked only a few yards bareheaded and had a severe fever as a result. A man lost his hat when his boat overturned and, although he covered his head with his shirt, it was too late and he had a severe sunstroke. It was much too easy to reach death's door by a little carelessness.

The doctor had hoped he could avoid performing a major operation until he was properly equipped. He had no such luck and his first strangulated hernia was done in great haste, using Dr. Christol's boys' bedroom as an operation theater. A missionary acted as his assistant and all went well, but it was a relief to know that such an experience need not be repeated.

The patients showed so much confidence in the doctor, however, that they submitted to any treatment without alarm. Luckily, he had so far lost no cases following operations, and one girl wrote in a letter to a Sunday School pen pal in Europe, "with the Doctor here wonderful things happen. He kills sick people and cures them and then awakens them again." The Africans could not understand anesthesia at all and thought it was the same as being dead. One small boy had to be brought to the doctor by force because he thought he was going to be eaten. He had heard about cannibals and thought he was to end in a cooking pot.

Most of the patients have been very grateful and one who had recovered after treatment for a strangulated hernia, the operation most often needed in the tropical forests, collected twenty francs from his relatives to give the doctor in payment for the "expensive thread" used in sewing him up, while the uncle of a boy who had been cured of sores gave fourteen days of work to the hospital in appreciation.

Trips up the river to care for a missionary or one of his family who was ill sometimes took the Schweitzers, as doctor and nurse, on a canoe journey lasting several days. On one such trip they spent two days at the mission at Samkita where only a short while before a leopard had killed twenty-two hens and at another time several of the mission goats. On this particular trip the Schweitzers tried their first monkey meat, which tasted much like

121

goat, although the couple disliked the idea inasmuch as it seemed too close to cannibalism.

The paddlers sometimes protested because Schweitzer was not a sportsman and a trip with him brought no excitement. He carried a gun but only to shoot snakes if the need arose. Shooting animals in the primeval forest was merely killing for the sake of killing, since the bodies can rarely be found afterward. This was against Albert's nature and principles. However, he often had his men stop paddling so that he could watch the animal life along the river.

Snakes were different and he often had to use his gun on them at his very doorstep. Poisonous snakes swarmed everywhere, even in the grass around his house, and there was a constant struggle to push the jungle back so as to keep them farther away. They entered any door left open, so everybody had to be careful that the houses were kept tightly closed. The creatures dropped from the trees onto the roofs at any time of the day or night. If they were rattlers that made a noise or were highly colored and easily seen, they were less feared, but unfortunately too many of them made no noise and looked like dead sticks. These were the most dangerous of all and everyone had to be constantly on the watch for them. Great boa constrictors often slipped into the hen house and became so swollen with the hens they ate that they couldn't get out again. This was generally the sign for a feast, for the natives like the meat of the boa and both patients and school chil-

dren always fought for a small piece. These large snakes can even swallow a goat whole!

Natives are more aware of snakes and spot them more easily than white men can, but Dr. Schweitzer soon learned to be always on the watch and quick with a gun. He learned, too, that in Africa no one puts a hand into a drawer without first looking inside carefully, for scorpions, centipedes and poisonous insects are too likely to be there, ready to sting or bite a careless person.

Often at night herds of large elephants raided with disastrous results the banana plantations which furnished the hospital with its main source of food for the patients. The natives mainly subsist on bananas and manioc and very little else, so that malnutrition is rife. These two plants, however, are the only ones that supply food all the year round and so have become very important. Manioc is a large root which is poisonous unless it is soaked for a long time in running water. Then it is crushed into a sort of dough, rolled in leaves, and cooked so as to become a kind of bread. Bananas, however, exhaust the soil after three years of continual growth and the natives find it necessary to make new plantings constantly. Yet wherever they can succeed in clearing the land and planting banana and manioc they are assured of a good food supply, so long as they keep out weeds, wild boars and elephants.

Unfortunately, no food can be stored or kept for very long in that region. Neither potatoes nor rice will grow, nor will corn nor peas, while the breadfruit trees bear fruit only between October and June. Consequently, the hospital garden assumes a vital importance to health, particularly in the case of white persons. If at the beginning of the dry season in June the garden is planted with beans, cabbage, radishes and carrots, and the daily watering is properly supervised and the weeds are kept out, a good garden crop is ready in no time. Oranges ripen in April and are both welcome and needed. Flour, rice and sugar have to be imported. So must milk, since cows are soon killed by the sleeping sickness carried by the tsetse fly and goats find it hard to survive the mange. Existence for the whites is by no means easy. The natives have less difficulty for the forest gives them wood, bamboo and raffia leaves for their huts, and with a little fishing and hunting added to their supplies of manioc and banana they get along fairly well. The native is driven to employment only when he needs something for which he must pay money, such as a wife, an ax or a music box. As a rule he lives happily in his village in a forest clearing or along the bank of a river, not idle but free most of the time to do as he pleases.

He is free in the sense of being his own master but not free from illness, as was evident from the doctor's busy life. And because Dr. Schweitzer felt that his patients should give in proportion to their abilities, he had them make gifts of poultry, eggs, bananas or money; for with the money thus collected he could buy rice with which to supplement their supply of food. If they were fit to help with work while they waited for treatment, they did so, and so did the families who brought the patients into the hospital and had to wait until they were well enough to be taken home again. Yet they only worked as long as they were being watched, and so for days Dr. Schweitzer had to keep on leaving his sick patients to superintend the building of a hut on the far side of the river for sleeping sickness victims.

Treating patients with sleeping sickness took much of his time for he found it a common and dangerous disease. There was a time when sleeping sickness was not as widespread through Central Africa as it is now, for there was little traveling from one territory to another. When a group from the coast wished to trade with people toward the interior, they went only as far as the border of their country to meet the traders, for to venture further was to be eaten. Europeans came and natives began to move about as crews on their boats, carrying the sleeping sickness, if they had it, into new territory. The tsetse fly spread the dreaded disease from person to person and the inhabitants died in large numbers. When the patients were brought to the hospital they usually had very high fever and often had become mentally deranged, for that is the course the disease frequently takes before the actual sleeping condition sets in. Often two or three years pass before the patient begins to sleep every time he sits down. At last the sleep is so deep that he cannot be awakened. He becomes nothing but skin and bones and is covered with bedsores; death is slow in coming. Often by the time the patient arrived at the Schweitzer hospital it was too late to do anything, for early detection is the only chance of recovery.

There was too little time for the long laboratory examination of the blood needed to detect the disease in its earliest stages and there were always long lines of waiting patients to be seen, surgical dressings to be changed, sores to be washed out, medicine to be mixed and distributed. Sleeping sickness was only one of the doctor's worries—there were malaria patients to be treated and lepers were far too common and at that time there was nothing known to help the sufferers. Dysentary was always present—a menace if not cared for at once—and operations, especially those of strangulated hernia, must be performed every few days.

The doctor always quieted a patient as Mrs. Schweitzer prepared the anaesthetic and Joseph, wearing long rubber gloves, got ready to assist. "You'll go to sleep and in a while you'll wake up and the pain will be gone. Don't be afraid!" He would say and the patient was assured. Hours later, in the dark dormitory, the doctor watched while his patient wakened and heard him say, "There is no pain. Thank you, thank you, Doctor!" Then the doctor would reply, loud enough for all to hear, "It was the love of Jesus that told the doctor and his wife to come to Africa to help the suffering natives. It is this love which makes white people give their money to keep the doctor and his wife there and sends them medicine and bandages." At such times Dr. Schweitzer feels the true meaning of brotherhood as Jesus meant it.

127

The Schweitzers could never forget that their hospital stood at the edge of the jungle, for all around them lived panthers, leopards, apes, elephants, buffalo and snakes, while hippos and crocodiles ruled the river, making travel by canoe hazardous. Patients were always arriving who had been bitten by a chimpanzee or a gorilla or a monkey, for these are the real rulers of the jungle. From the very beginning, Albert Schweitzer felt he was an intruder or at least no more than a guest in their country. He treated all life as sacred and destroyed it only when it endangered another life. He always gave a present to any native who saved the life of a young or injured wild animal by bringing it to the hospital. Soon the number of pets around the hospital had increased substantially. Fi-fi, a baby chimp, was only a few days old when she arrived and had to be fed by bottle. Baby antelopes, Leonie and Theodore, who had to be fed by medicine dropper, were welcome additions to the menagerie. White persons returning to Europe presented their pets, knowing they would find a good home. None was turned away. Dr. Schweitzer continued to preach and practice a reverence for all life, and the value of life in general. Yet on occasion jungle creatures could be great pests and the greatest of these was the traveler ant.

At the beginning and end of the rainy season the traveler ants go on the warpath and the Schweitzer cottage lay right across the line of march. During these migrations several columns of ants, with five or six abreast, moved along at great speed, in never-ending lines. On one occa-

sion, Dr. Schweitzer noted that a column continued to pass for thirty-six hours! When they came to a path, the ants of the warrior caste stood aside, facing outward, ready to fight any intruder, while the remaining ants with their brood passed safely between. A column may suddenly and for no apparent reason disperse over the surrounding territory and any unfortunate living thing caught within the area is quickly devoured by thousands of the small, vicious creatures.

One night the Schweitzers heard a queer noise coming from the hen house. The doctor rushed out to free the chickens for the ants were already getting into their nostrils and eyes and were killing them. Mrs. Schweitzer sounded the bugle, which quickly brought men from the hospital with buckets of water into which the doctor poured Lysol. Then, while his wife held a lantern, he poured the deadly solution all about the house as their only safeguard. During the ant's migrations this could happen two or three nights in a single week. It was merely one of the trials of living at the edge of the jungle. Yet the beauty of the birds and the butterflies was breathtaking, for nowhere is there such color as you can find in the jungle, and both the wildness and the beauty made Albert Schweitzer feel privileged to be among them.

Out of this closeness of living with the untamed and beautiful tropical nature and with the everpresent suffering of both animals and human beings grew his greatest qualities—the feeling that all life has value and meaning and his deep sympathy with all who suffer. Here at the jungle's edge he could practice the teaching of Jesus that all men are brothers and should love one another. And he found joy in being able to ease pain, feeling that the strong should help the weak and those who have been spared pain should help relieve the pain of others.

CHAPTER 10

Prisoners of War

THE weather in Africa follows a well defined pattern of wet and dry seasons and the Schweitzers soon learned what to expect. The long dry season lasts from June to September and the short dry season from December through January. In between it rains. However, the rain does not fall continuously and usually hard rains each night are followed by beautiful days. Christmas is the hottest time of the year. Then the humidity is intolerable and not a leaf stirs. Heavy rains cause the rivers to rise but, since the hospital and missionary buildings are on the hills, no harm comes to them. In April, the citrus fruits begin to ripen. In May, a very slight breeze appears and occasionally short wind storms which they call "tornadoes." In June, at the beginning of the dry season, the gardens are planted, so long as the seeds have not spoiled from all the dampness. No time can be lost, since the growing season is very short and the vegetables must be ready before the rainy season starts again. The sand banks begin to show as the water in the river drops, and by August fish are easily caught in nets in the shallow waters.

131

The jungle is always green. Leaves fall all the time and new ones are growing. Even during the dry season, the ground remains moist and the grass is never dry. The evening sky glows with the burning of trees, for only at this time of year can the natives hope to clear the ground for new banana plantations. Fire is their only way of making a clearing, for they have no tools. Even if the natives had tools, they would find the work of felling trees too hard and they would not know what to do with the wood that was cut. Furthermore, the soil is richer for the ashes it receives from the burning. The African way is for the men to clear and the women to till and harvest. Albert Schweitzer hated to think of the animals and plants that were destroyed by the flames, yet he accepted the burnings as necessary. At the end of the season, in September, the rains commence again, the humidity rises, and the heat once more becomes almost insufferable.

When their first Christmas came around, Dr. and Mrs. Schweitzer placed their green and red twisted candles on a palm tree instead of on their customary fir tree, and they were homesick for the snow-covered fields and woods of their homeland. They longed for the quiet of winter when all nature takes a rest, for the perpetual riotous African nature was tiring to anyone accustomed to seasons of growth and rest.

Yet Albert Schweitzer found rest in his music. At first he thought that his work in Africa would put an end to his life as a musician. He felt that, if he allowed his fingers and his feet to become rusty, he would be able to forget about his music. Yet somehow he could not keep away from his piano after a long, tiring day at the hospital. One evening, after a particularly hard day, he sat down to play Bach's organ fugues and his mind went back to Paris and to the cathedral music and to Widor, his teacher with whom he had spent so many memorable hours. He realized that he need not get rusty, even if he was in the African jungle, and he decided to use every moment he could find from his work to perfect his techniques. He would practice one great composition after another until he knew them from memory and could play them to his complete satisfaction. And all of this he did, first Bach, then Mendelssohn and later on Widor and Franck. Furthermore, he made steady progress because there were no concerts to have to prepare for, no hurry, and even a half hour at the piano with its organ foot pedals made him feel he had accomplished something and gave him a feeling of recreation as well.

Albert Schweitzer was not at all surprised that he had a common understanding with the missionaries in the field, for they were all busy trying to put into practice the teachings of Jesus and his companions found joy in sharing their work for the brotherhood of man. Before long he was invited to take part in the preaching, which he gladly did, and his religious services to this day follow the pattern he started forty years ago. Every Sunday the services are held in the open, with the families of the sick, together with many of the patients often busy around their cooking fires or just squatting on the ground. Animals and children run freely about. Dr. Schweitzer, using the very simple words of Jesus or Paul, stands with an interpreter on either side, translating his sermon sentence by sentence into the two native dialects most commonly understood.

Once when he was invited to attend a conference of missionaries, Schweitzer was asked to give his opinion on some matter which was being discussed. He did so freely, but when he had finished a native Negro preacher spoke up and said, "The doctor is not a theologian as we are and this matter is entirely outside his experience." Albert Schweitzer was pleased because then he realized that he had successfully kept his promise to the Paris Committee to work only as a medical doctor and not to promote his own views concerning Christian beliefs.

During his first year in Africa, the busy doctor found that the days were never long enough to ease the pain of the suffering bodies brought to him for treatment. Yet all too soon and suddenly he was to find his work cut short and that he had all of his time on his hands, instead of a half hour taken here and there, for just sixteen months after his arrival, in Africa, the unbelievable happened and the First World War broke out. Alsace was then a part of Germany and, because the Schweitzers were German citizens, they were made prisoners of war on the fifth of August, 1914. Negro guards arrived to carry out orders and see to it that the prisoners had no contact whatsoever with the white missionaries or the natives and that they remained in their own house.

134

The Negro natives of Lambaréné could not understand why their beloved doctor was a prisoner and they came from long distances to abuse the poor guards for acting as though they were his masters. All the natives knew of the war was that prices of articles in the store were now much higher and that there was no more work for them in the timber trade. One old Negro heard that ten white men who used to work in the district had been killed in battle and asked, "How will they ever be able to pay for the dead?" for in Africa a person who is killed must be paid for. The killer gives money or presents to the family of the dead. Then again he asked, "Why don't all the tribes meet and have a palaver (discussion)?" He came to his own conclusion that "people of Europe kill just to be cruel, for of course they did not wish to eat all those dead!" One thing that the natives did understand, although not the reason for it, was that the good doctor was not permitted to help them when they needed him.

For a while Albert Schweitzer, who had been working under pressure for so many years, did not know what to do with so much leisure time. Since he could not go to the hospital to work, what could he do?—Music?—Finish the the book he was writing on Paul? With the world in a mess and civilization crumbling, he could not bring himself to do either. His mind turned more and more to the reasons for the war. The European civilization was going to pieces for the lack of a good, workable code of ethics or behavior.

For some time now the state of society had been worrying him and more and more he had felt a need to express his thoughts. So now, with paper and pencil, he started to write a criticism and appraisal of civilization. It seemed strange to be able to write, hour after hour, without interruption, yet at first that is just what he did. In his enthusiasm for writing, he did not see the antelope which came into his room to visit. The antelope was inquisitive and when Dr. Schweitzer noticed the animal it had already eaten part of the manuscript he had been writing. After that he hung his papers on nails above his desk, well out of reach. And, being the kind of person he was, he also arranged for a native to go into the jungle to gather fresh leaves to supplement the animal's food.

After a while, both the white and black people, began to protest to the authorities against the order which made it impossible for them to see the doctor when he was the only one within hundreds of miles. And every day the commandant had to issue many notes, asking the guards to allow someone to see the doctor because he needed medical help.

By the end of November, Widor in Paris managed to secure the release of the Schweitzers from their internment, and once again they were able to go about their work in the hospital, although with heavy hearts and with the fear that their medical supplies would run out, for they could see no end to the conflict in Europe. Their own families and friends at home were under fire and they were concerned for them too.

Still Dr. Schweitzer continued to find some time every

day to go on with his writing; often far into the night his lamp could be seen burning as he struggled to put his thoughts into words. At last, in 1915, he realized that he should not limit his effort to an explanation of what was happening only in terms of past history but he should be able to offer something helpful and constructive as well. And until he could think of a remedy for the sickness of civilization, he felt rather like a man who has lost his boat and doesn't know how to build another one.

When the Christmas candles on their palm tree were half burned through, Dr. Schweitzer blew them out. They were all the Schweitzers had and they could not tell for how long they would be cut off from Europe. They could no longer afford to give rice to the sick, because it was running short. Newspapers were long in coming and they felt completely isolated from the rest of the world. Dr. Schweitzer did his best to keep any illustrated papers which came to the mission from reaching the natives so that they would not be able to picture the horror of white man's warfare. For the natives were deeply puzzled that the white men who came to them to teach them about love and brotherhood should be killing one another. How could people who knew and taught the commandments of Jesus act in such a way? And they were deeply troubled.

The following Christmas, the remaining halves of the candles were burned on the little palm tree that decorated the Schweitzer's house. The year which followed was difficult. The hospital work became increasingly hard. So many white people were now suffering because they had

had to stay too long in the tropics. Even Dr. Schweitzer's bedroom was used by his white patients, while he himself slept on the verandah, in a corner which had been covered with mosquito netting so that he could write out of doors whenever he had the time.

Joseph left. He could no longer be paid his usual seventy francs a month and the doctor was forced to cut it in half. This hurt the African's dignity and he left, making the Schweitzers' work very difficult indeed, for Joseph had served both as an interpreter and as a medical assistant and he could not be replaced.

The doctor and his wife began to show signs of the usual anemia and accompaning fatigue which affects white people who remain too long in the tropics. Walking up the hill from the hospital to the house was quite exhausting, yet Dr. Schweitzer retained the same mental freshness he had always possessed. He was able to write on his *Philos ophy of Civilization* and play his piano, and these diver sions relaxed him as they had always done!

His mind worked continually on the burden of civiliza tion and its obligations to relieve suffering. He came to the conclusion that all who had experienced pain and anguish belonged to a fellowship united together by the bonds of suffering which obligated them to help others who were in pain. And in his own daily work he saw so much pain that the thought of it never really left his mind. One day while he was thinking along these lines he was summoned to visit the sick wife of the missionary at N'Gomo. No time could be lost and the only way to cover the miles quickly enough was to catch the river boat, just leaving the dock with a heavy barge in tow. He jumped into the boat without stopping to take any food along, but the natives on board shared their food with him. All he had to do throughout the day was to sit on the deck and think. It was a slow journey, for the season was dry and the river was low. So for three days Albert Schweitzer covered his note paper which he always carried with his thoughts, simply to keep his mind working in an orderly manner. Then, just at sunset when the boat was passing slowly through a herd of hippopotami, the words "reverence for life" came to his mind and it was as though a gate had been opened. Now he had an expression which included a positive way of thinking about all life.

Before long Mrs. Schweitzer began to be in very bad health and during the rainy season of 1916-1917 the doctor and his wife went to Cape Lopez, to stay in the empty house of a timber merchant. In return for the man's kindness, Dr. Schweitzer rolled heavy logs out of the water onto the shore.

When September came the couple returned to Lambaréné, much improved in health. They had no sooner recommenced their work at the hospital than they received an order to pack at once and leave on the next boat for Europe, as prisoners of war.

Frantically, they put the medicines and drugs in cases and stored them in a corrugated iron building. Then Mrs. Schweitzer packed their personal belongings for travel and some medicines, in case of need. Dr. Schweitzer made an outline in French of his book on civilization so that he could carry on with his writing if he ever got a chance. He left his manuscript with one of the missionaries, who promised to send it to him when the war was over. The process of packing was interrupted by an operation on a native for strangulated hernia, and then the Schweitzers hurried down to the river boat. The Father Superior of the Catholic Mission across the river came over to bid them farewell and to thank them for the work they had done in Africa. The natives wept as they waved good-bye, for they could not understand what was happening to their "Doctor Father."

At Cape Lopez, the Schweitzers were offered money by the husband of a former patient, but the gold they had brought over with them in case of war was now changed into French notes and Mrs. Schweitzer had sewn them into the linings of their clothes.

On the ship, the couple received good service from a steward who had been asked by a friend to help Dr. Schweitzer, if he ever had a chance, since the doctor had once cured him of sickness. Yet they were allowed to talk to no one and were taken on deck by a guard once every day for exercise. It was impossible to write under such circumstances and Albert Schweitzer concentrated on memorizing Widor's *Sixth Symphony* and several of Bach's fugues by using a table as an imaginary keyboard and the floor as pedals.

When the Schweitzers arrived at the port of Bordeaux on the west coast of France they were interned in a soldiers' barracks and here the doctor developed dysentery. He treated himself and improved somewhat. The two had orders to be ready to leave at any moment but had not fully understood and when they were awakened in the middle of the night, nothing had been packed and it was difficult to hurry with only a candle with which to see what they were doing. The guards were abusive and thought they were disobeying an order, but finally they pitied the couple and came in to help them push their things into their bags.

When they arrived at their prison in the mountainous country of the Pyrenees, an officer found a copy of the *Politics of Aristotle* among Dr. Schweitzer's belongings and expressed surprise that he was so dumb as to bring a political book into a prison camp. Dr. Schweitzer explained that the book was written long before the birth of Christ. The officer consulted a superior and found it was true enough, so he returned the book saying, "You can keep your book for we talk politics differently today."

In the courtyard of the prison, a guard approached and asked if he could do anything to serve Dr. Schweitzer, because the doctor had once cured his wife, and as a result Dr. Schweitzer was supplied with a table on which he could continue his "organ practice." He could play Bach silently on the table top, his power of concentration was so great.

Interned with the Schweitzers was a group of gypsies, the leader of whom asked Dr. Schweitzer if he was the musician mentioned in the book, *Musicians of Today*. When he received an affirmative answer, the gypsy asked the doctor to practice with the gypsy musicians, who had been allowed to keep their instruments and had been given an attic in which to play. When Mrs. Schweitzer awakened on her birthday, it was to a serenade by the gypsy band. Dr. Schweitzer himself soon became a busy man, for, since he was the only medical man among the prisoners, he was given a room and a job almost at once. As formerly, his days became very full, inasmuch as he now started to write again, as well as to practice his music whenever his medical duties allowed him the time for it.

After the Schweitzers had spent a long winter in prison, the spring of 1918 arrived, and with it came orders to transfer the couple to St. Remy, in Provence. They begged to stay where they were, and the governor of the prison also asked for them to remain, but orders were orders and they were transferred to St. Remy, where Alsatian prisoners were being kept. When they walked into the large common room of the prison, the ugliness of it seemed familiar. Dr. Schweitzer felt he had seen it before, the iron stove, the stovepipe, the walls—but where? Then he remembered they were all in a painting of Van Gogh's which had been made while the artist was there as a mental patient. The painter too had sat in this ugly room, only partly warmed by the stove, and had known the cold wind and the chilly stone floors and the walled-in garden. Mrs. Schweitzer was almost ill from the disagreeable weather and her husband, weakened from dysentery, was far from well. When the stronger prisoners were taken for a walk in the country, they tried to walk as fast and as far as possible, so the Schweitzers had to join the old and weak who went out for only a short walk with the governor of St. Remy.

Then in July a list was sent to St. Remy of the prisoners who were to be exchanged. Mrs. Schweitzer was ill and very homesick and her husband could not bring himself to tell her that her name was on the list but his was not. But during the night of July 12 the two were awakened and told to get packed at once. This time the list included Dr. Schweitzer's name as well as his wife's. And so they left.

At the Swiss border their train waited until the one carrying prisoners which were to be exchanged arrived and then they moved on toward Zurich. They could not see enough of the countryside with its clean houses and its fields of grain. At Zurich, they were met by old friends who had known for a long time that they would be on that train. When the Schweitzers first arrived in Alsace, they were shocked at the condition of their homeland. Mrs. Schweitzer went on to her parents at Strasbourg, while her husband remained at Constance, to complete the formalities. When he finally reached the old city, all was in darkness, for no lights were allowed in the streets. There was no use in attempting to reach the home of his wife's parents in the suburbs, so he searched in the darkness until he found the familiar house of a friend near St. Thomas's, where he spent the night.

Albert had hoped to visit his father at Günsbach, but Günsbach was within the battle ground and it was only

143

with much difficulty that he received permission to go there. Trains ran only as far as Colmar and from there the doctor had to walk the remaining ten miles on foot. Barbed wire and barricades were along every road, gun emplacements everywhere, houses were in ruins and in the distance he could hear the sound of gunfire. He found his father still the center of his flock. The old man had long since refused to go down to his cellar every time there was a bombardment but sat on, working in his study. Before long Mrs. Schweitzer also found her way to Günsbach, for she was worried concerning her husband's condition. At the end of August, Albert Schweitzer had an attack of pain and high fever and he realized that an operation was necessary. He could hardly walk without his wife's help, but together they managed to cover four miles before they were picked up by a car and driven to Colmar. They finally reached Strasbourg and the hospital and the operation took place the first of September.

When he was strong enough after his operation, Albert accepted an appointment as doctor in the city hospital and at the same time became once more curate of St. Nichols, so the Schweitzers were able to move into the parsonage on the St. Nicholas Embankment. This employment was a great relief, for Dr. Schweitzer had not known how they were going to live, let alone pay off the debts he had incurred during the past three years on behalf of his hospital in Africa.

CHAPTER 11

Lectures, Concerts and Honors

W ITH the armistice at the end of the First World War, Alsace passed from German to French rule, and during the following two years Albert Schweitzer frequently crossed the border with a rucksack full of food to send to friends who were starving in Germany, for it was a time of great trouble.

The Schweitzers settled down in the parsonage and Albert carried on his medical and preaching jobs with some difficulty, since he had not fully recovered from his operation. On his forty-fourth birthday, on January 14, 1919, their baby daughter Rhena was born.

At first, Albert Schweitzer devoted his late evenings to study and playing Bach's preludes, in preparation for writing his final three volumes on Bach's works. He put this aside, however, to work on his book on civilization, but while he waited for the first part of the manuscript to arrive from Lambaréné, where he had left it with the missionary, he began to make a study of the other great religions of the world—Judaism, Islam, Buddhism, Brahminism and Hinduism, and the religious thinking of the Chinese. He came to the conclusion that civilization everywhere was based upon acceptance of an ethical code of behavior, of a recognition of man's relationship and responsibility to his fellow man.

During the following summer Schweitzer had to have a second operation since he had not regained his strength as readily as he should. He longed for contact once again with the artistic world, and when October came he got enough money together to travel to Barcelona, in Spain, to give an organ concert. He realized then that he was still sufficiently a musician to be of some value. He was surprised and pleased when he was asked to deliver a series of lectures at Upsala University in Sweden, even though he had not been in touch with the educational world since 1913. His manuscript for the first part of his book on civilization had not yet left Africa, so he had to rewrite it, since he needed the whole of it for his lectures. He was thankful that he had made a hurried outline before he left Lambaréné as a prisoner of war. The missing part did arrive finally, but not until after he had returned from Sweden.

In Sweden, during Eastertime of 1920, he put into words the thoughts that had been in his mind for years. He led up finally to his concept of "Reverence for Life." When he presented this in his last lecture, he was so emotionally tense he could hardly speak.

Dr. and Mrs. Schweitzer were guests at the Archbishop's house. The air of Sweden was completely refreshing and before Albert's stay was ended he became a well man again, filled with his old strength and his joy in work.

With his health regained, the worry concerning how he was to repay the wartime debts of his African hospital rose to plague him once more. One day, while walking with the Swedish archbishop, he spoke of his burden and his inability to see a solution to his problem. The Archbishop suggested that the doctor give some public lectures about his hospital while he was in Sweden, for that neutral country had grown rich during the war and the people had money to spend and would welcome hearing of such things. He even knew of a young theological student who would serve as an interpreter. Dr. Schweitzer was enthusiastic and at once started to prepare his talks. How glad he was that he had mastered the technique of speaking through an interpreter. He spoke in short, clear sentences which the student translated so quickly that the audience soon forgot they were hearing a translation. Everywhere the people were keenly interested in hearing about Schweitzer's work in Africa and he relived it himself in the telling. He gave organ recitals as well and found the old Swedish organs wonderfully suited to the music of Bach. In a few weeks of lectures and concerts he earned enough money to pay off all the hospital debts.

At last, fully recovered in health, and happy in a new resolution to return to Africa as soon as he could, Albert Schweitzer went back to Strasbourg and wrote a book about the hospital which was published first in Swedish, then in German and English, and later on in French,

Dutch, Danish and Finnish. Very soon the whole world was to know of the hospital at the Edge of the Primeval Forest, and about the Dr. Schweitzer who had built it up.

By the spring of 1921, Albert Schweitzer realized that, while he had been willing to sacrifice all his music and academic work and financial independence in order to serve the suffering natives in Africa, this sacrifice was not actually necessary. Because of his practice in Africa, on the piano given him by his friends in Paris, he was better able, rather than less, to interpret the work of the great composers. Now, through his lectures, he was able to teach as well. He found that he could support his wife and child—and also earn enough money for his hospital—with his music and his pen. As a result, in April 1921 he resigned his posts as preacher at St. Nicholas and doctor at the city hospital and took his family to his father's home at Günsbach. Here he could find the quiet he needed in which to write the *Philosophy of Civilization,* which was published two years later in two volumes.

The two years at Günsbach, however, were constantly interrupted with trips away to give lectures and recitals, for he was continually being reminded of the need to earn money for his hospital and for the support of his family when he should return to Africa. He visited Switzerland and Sweden again, then England, made another trip to Sweden and to Switzerland, and one to Prague.

During his visit to England, he went to City Temple, a church in London, to give a scheduled talk on his work in Africa and to show slides of the hospital and the natives.

With him went a young woman who translated his German into English in a fully packed church. When the lecture was over, the minister, Dr. F. W. Norwood, thanked him and as they started to the dining room to eat the dinner prepared by the ladies of the church, the minister told Dr. Schweitzer that two thousand people were outside and downstairs who had not heard him because there had not been enough room inside the church. "Why," said Dr. Schweitzer, "they shall hear the lecture. I will repeat it. Have them brought into the church!" The dinner was put back on the stove to keep warm and the jungle doctor and his interpréter repeated the lecture.

When it was over and again the group moved toward the dining room, someone asked, "Dr. Schweitzer, do you know that we have a fine organ in the church? It would be good to hear you play some Bach on it."

"Of course you shall! Where is the organ? Show me the way to the loft!" And so the dinner was once more put back to keep warm, while those inside the church were treated to a wonderful recital of Bach's music. At ten o'clock the party finally appeared in the dining room, where the patient ladies served the now much warmed-over dinner. But hardly had the doctor been served than he looked at his watch and exclaimed "What! After ten o'clock? I have made an appointment for ten!" And he hurriedly made his departure. He never spared himself, for he was again as strong as he ever had been and there were never enough hours in which to accomplish all he wanted to do.

In the autumn of 1923, Schweitzer corrected the proofs of his book on civilization and also wrote his memoirs of his childhood. Whenever he could spare a moment he spent it packing for his return to Africa. This time he would be going without his wife, for Mrs. Schweitzer was not too well and Rhena was too young to be taken to the tropics.

CHAPTER 12

Rebuilding the Jungle Hospital

THE sun was just rising as the river boat docked at
Lambaréné. It was Easter of 1924 and the doctor and a
young Oxford student named Noel Gillespie, who had
come out to help him, stepped ashore. Seven years had
gone by since Dr. Schweitzer had left as a prisoner of war
and much had happened in the meantime. More than
ever, he felt the absence of his helpmate who had planned
with him and worked with him and suffered with him in
this jungle spot.

The natives were there with canoes to take the doctor
to the mission a couple of miles upstream. The shore
looked just the same as when he last saw it. So did the
river itself, although this time he was not afraid of being
turned over into the water before they reached the mission
station. But at the mission settlement nothing was as he
had expected to find it. Tropical undergrowth covered the
land where the hospital had once stood. The corrugated
iron building which had been his operating room and
consulting room, and one other building, were still there

151

but without roofs. The path to his house had disappeared.

With a heavy heart, he tried to obtain workers who would help him rebuild, but the timber trade was so good anyone who could work at all was fully employed and none would give any time to the making of leaf tiles, which the natives made by stretching raffia leaves over bamboo rods, even when the tiles were for their own dilapidated huts.

So the very first day Dr. Schweitzer and Noel started off in a canoe to visit the native villages, in order to buy leaf tiles wherever they could be found. The doctor was joyously welcomed everywhere and he came back with sixty-four tiles, though only after giving a good many presents in payment. He even went so far as to threaten not to care for any sick persons a village might send him, unless he obtained some leaf tiles. But the natives knew their doctor and only laughed at the threat. With the sixty-four tiles, however, he was able to repair the roof of his house and to settle in for Easter.

Throughout the forest the tom-toms were busy sending out the beaten message that the doctor had returned. Patients began to arrive within the first few days and very soon the place was overflowing. Many were old people for whom nothing could be done. The rainy season was still at its height, the hospital had no roof, and every morning Dr. Schweitzer found most of his patients lying under their beds in an effort to keep dry. Because he was unable to hire anybody, he was forced to draft every able-bodied individual who accompanied the sick to the hospital.

To those who helped repair the buildings, he gave both food and gifts. The mornings he had to devote to attending the sick but the afternoons he assigned to supervising and helping with the process of reconstruction. Once when he was carrying a heavy load of wood out of the rain, he saw a Negro visiting a sick patient and called to him to help, but the reply was, "No, I am an intellectual and cannot carry wood!" To which the doctor answered, "I wanted to be one, too, but I didn't succeed."

Many river trips had to be taken to secure leaf tiles and hardwood timber. The native oarsmen always asked Schweitzer to tell them what was different in the white man's country, and they never tired of hearing the same

153

stories over and over again for they could not fully believe what they heard. The doctor told the Negroes that
in Europe there were great forest fires. His listeners could
not imagine a country where wood is always dry enough
to burn and they talked it over at great length. When this
conversation came to an end, Schweitzer told the boatmen
that white people row boats for pleasure, without receiving
pay or presents. This made them laugh, for they could
not conceive of any man rowing or paddling who didn't
have to go on a journey. They had no idea at all of what
sport meant or why a person could do anything just for
exercise. The doctor told them that in Europe a man
does not have to buy a wife—well, that was simply impossible, of course, for in Africa a woman has value and
her family sells her to a man and takes her back, if her
purchaser forgets or is unable to make a payment when it
falls due. In fact, parents start to pay for a wife for their
son as soon as he can walk, and a girl is often bought
when she is only a baby, although she remains in her own
home until she is mature. A girl belongs to her mother
and her mother's brothers and as such they receive the
money and take her back again if the occasion arises.

Where once the patients came from two African tribes,
Dr. Schweitzer now found them coming from as many as
ten different tribes, and some of these were very primitive.
The growing timber trade had drawn savages from the
deep interior of Africa, seeking work, and some of them
were extremely difficult to handle. The Bandjabi tribe
took no orders, obeyed no one and had no respect for

anything, least of all the possessions of other patients at the hospital. The doctor's hen house furnished stolen chicken for many of their cooking pots. Hospital rules meant nothing at all and, since they drank freely of polluted river water when they were thirsty, they soon spread dysentery through the hospital community. Once when Dr. Schweitzer found a patient drinking from the river, he said to Joseph, who had returned as assistant and interpreter, "I am a blockhead to come to Africa to help such savages!" Joseph replied, "Yes, Doctor, on earth you are a blockhead, but you are not a blockhead in heaven."

Dr. Schweitzer found he could no longer manage the hospital alone, so he sent to Europe for help and when the first doctor, Dr. Nessman, arrived he was given the medical side of the hospital to run, allowing Schweitzer to work as a full-time builder. More buildings were urgently needed and it was also vital that a strong room be built for the mentally ill, who were brought to Dr. Schweitzer in chains. Often he had to send them away because there was no place to keep them. Also a cottage was needed at once for white patients, for there was no further room for them and still they continued to come. The living standards of the two races are so different that naturally they need separate quarters.

A nurse came along with Dr. Nessman. So much responsibility fell to her that it soon became apparent to the doctors that they must have more assistance. Once again a call for help was sent out. This brought another

doctor and nurse from Europe. The doctor had special-
ized in surgery and the nurse was particularly trained in
caring for the sick. Dr. Schweitzer spent more and more
of his time directing the work of the natives and doing
actual carpentry himself.

A motor boat named *Task sa mycket,* meaning many
thanks, arrived as a gift from friends in Sweden, and later
on another one was sent from Jutland, in Denmark. No
gifts were ever so helpful. By the autumn of 1925 the
forest hospital was more than rebuilt and Dr. Schweitzer
was beginning to think that he could start to write a long-
planned book on the Apostle Paul. Then suddenly catas-
trophe struck the hospital!

Because the natives had been so busy working in the
timber industry, they had not bothered to clear ground
and plant their banana and manioc. They were content
with polished rice and canned food, all of it deficient in
vitamins. They had neither the right kind of food nor by
any means enough of it. Many were starving and then
an epidemic of dysentery began. The hospital was soon
filled with the sick and the dying, with nothing to feed
them. The doctors and nurses were kept busy day and
night and the motorboats were out every day, searching for
places where rice could be bought for the hospital community.

Slowly it dawned on Dr. Schweitzer that he must move
everything to a place where the hospital could spread out,
since all the land the mission could let them have was
fully occupied. There was room only for about fifty

patients, whereas one hundred and fifty were present to be taken care of all the time. The present situation was impossible!

He had ordered iron roofing to replace the leaf tiles which were needing to be repaired and replaced all the time and were becoming harder and harder to obtain. And he realized that he would only be postponing the inevitable, if he put the new roofing on the old building. A move was essential, not only for the sake of the natives but for the increasing numbers of white people who were coming to Africa and to his hospital for care. He had to make a place for them and for the doctors and nurses and native orderlies so necessary to the running of the hospital. He had planned to leave the staff to carry on without him for a time while he returned to Europe to see his wife and daughter and to raise funds with which to support the hospital. But when the famine and epidemic broke out, he called the doctors and nurses together and told them of his idea of moving the hospital to another place, about two miles upstream. They too had begun to realize the impossible nature of the existing situation and knew that it would only become worse unless something drastic was done.

The land was obtained and Dr. Schweitzer became a full-time director of native labor. He now could get help, for when people are starving and payment is made in food, they will work—in this case, if directed and watched. The other three doctors assisted in the clearing whenever they had time, while the nurses became excellent overseers of native clearers and planters. Planting the garden was the most urgent part of the project. Dr. Schweitzer visualized a garden where there would be enough fruit and vegetables for all. In the course of clearing the new ground, he found many oil palms, which were carefully transplanted, since palm oil is their only source of fats. Oil is pressed from the fruit and then the nuts are exported, since further oil can be extracted from the kernels. Mango trees and oil palms had been introduced from other countries and planted around the native villages, and from there the seeds had been carried by parrots far and wide through the jungle and up and down the African coast.

The doctor had gained much valuable experience from having had to rebuild the old original hospital on his return after the war, so all that effort was not wasted. The new hut for the sleeping sickness patients was supposedly being built. Men had been assigned to the work. Yet when Dr. Schweitzer went over in the evening of the first day to see how it was progressing, he found nothing had been done. He was furious and began to express his feelings concerning the undependability of the natives, when a young Negro said, "Doctor, it is not our fault but yours. If you go to treat the sick at the hospital, we are alone and we can do nothing, but if you stay with us, we will work." That was another valuable lesson learned which Dr. Schweitzer remembered through all his later years in Africa. When he set a workman to build a hut, he stayed to see that it was done. Although it annoyed him to have to do so, it was the only way. Other things irritated him, particularly when they interfered with the general progress of the hospital. Every African Negro is surrounded by a set of taboos—beliefs in things to be avoided or not to be done for fear of harm or death. Among the people of the Pahouin tribe, for instance, if a wife is expecting a child, her husband must not fill a hole with soil, drive nails, or step over a procession of ants. And a procession of ants might hold up a man for days. No wonder that these and other taboos interfered with getting things done!

Taboos often got in the way of the doctor's operations. A woman who was very ill and needed an operation refused to allow Dr. Schweitzer to do it, which was most unusual, since the faith the natives have in their doctor is such that, as a rule, they allow him to do anything. He discovered that two men had "cast a spell" on her which said that she would die if she was ever cut by a knife. However, he finally persuaded her to be operated on and within a few days she was well enough to go home.

Patients pay no attention to what they are told and will lift a bandage to feel the operation wound. Germs have no meaning for them at all. A day after an operation they will bathe in the dirty river or they will eat their fill of fruit just before the time for a stomach operation, or immediately after. Always there must be a constant watch or they will kill themselves through ignorance.

It would be impossible to describe in detail all of the work which went into the clearing of the land, the hunting for hardwood in the forest, the charring of the beams to make them insect proof. All of the last had to be done by

159

Dr. Schweitzer, since the natives could not be trusted to char the wood without burning it all the way through, nor could the natives hold the beams straight when setting them up. At the time that Dr. Schweitzer was working as a builder, with no energy left at the end of the day to do any writing, he received word that he had been given an honorary degree by the University of Prague!

At the end of January in 1927, the move to the new hospital was finally made. The patients were filled with joy at the light and space and cool air of the new buildings. Their families were pleased with their huts. Now there was room for growth and expansion. As the doctor made his nightly rounds, the patients thanked him from behind their mosquito nets, and, for the first time since he had come to Africa, he felt that his patients were housed like human beings.

Finally, he set to work to tear down the old buildings, so that he could use the materials over again. He built an isolation hospital for dysentery and a hut for mental patients. At last he had a hospital equipped to take care of two hundred patients. In July 1927, he was free to plan his return to Europe, where he could rejoin his family, find a much needed rest, and be restored by his music and his writing.

CHAPTER 13

Second World War

ALBERT SCHWEITZER spent two years in Europe and they were busy ones. He took his wife and child to Konigsberg, a mountain resort in the Black Forest, where he established a summer house. In this quiet and restful place, he wrote more on his book about Paul, although he was continually leaving to give lectures and recitals, visiting Sweden, Holland, Denmark, Germany, Switzerland, Czechoslovakia and England. Everywhere he went he met old friends and made new ones. He also had to find new doctors and nurses who would go to Africa, for some of those he had left behind at Lambaréné had been compelled to return to Europe, either because of illness or from family concern, and the hospital could not remain shorthanded.

In the summer of 1928, he went to Frankfurt in Germany to receive the Goethe Prize for his studies of the great philosopher and poet and to deliver a lecture on his debt to that great German poet whom he had always admired so much. With the prize money he was able to build a home of his own in the village of Günsbach. He called it *The Home That Goethe Built.* The old house in which he had spent his happy childhood was now occupied by the new village pastor, for his father had died. Yet Albert's roots had grown so deep in this part of the country that he needed to feel his home was still there, and from his new house at the edge of the village he had a clear view of his beloved Munster valley. However, he did not actually use the Goethe Prize money for this purpose until he had succeeded in earning a similar amount for his hospital fund. Nowadays, the Günsbach house is used as a rest place for workers from the hospital and as general headquarters for the Lambaréné hospital as a whole, with a full-time secretary to carry on the business when Dr. Schweitzer himself is away.

With so many lectures and recitals to be given in order to earn enough money to keep the hospital going, in addition to the time taken in finding new workers to go out to Africa and the business of building the Günsbach house, it is no wonder that when the day came for his return to Africa the doctor's book on St. Paul was not finished. He completed the last chapter on the boat that was taking him to Africa for the third time, although on this occasion he was no longer alone, for his wife accompanied him, together with several new workers for the hospital. They left their daughter in a school in Switzerland. With never a minute to be lost, he wrote the introduction to his book after he had boarded the little river steamer on the day after Christmas. When the boat reached the hospital landing, the book was finished and

he was able once more to give the whole of his mind to
his African adventure.

As usual, he was faced with the need for more buildings and he started at once to construct another ward for

the very sick patients and a new mental ward. Next came a large theft-proof storehouse and a house for native orderlies. A new wharf was built and also a road and a concrete reservoir for rain, and a concrete dining room and common room. It was hard work but this time Schweitzer had the help of several doctors, nurses and technicians, so that at the end of the day there was still energy left to continue with his music and his writing. He found rest from his activities as a medical man and builder in turning to write his biography which he called *Out of My Life and Thoughts*.

Also, as usual, the hospital grounds were full of hens, geese, turkeys, antelopes, monkeys, chimpanzees, not to mention cats and dogs. Mrs. Schweitzer declared there were already more than enough and that Albert should not add to this menagerie without her consent. He promised, but no sooner had she left on a short trip up the river when a native came to him with a wild hog which she said was so tame that all Dr. Schweitzer needed to do was to call "Josephine!" and the animal would run to him and follow him about like a dog. It did! And because he could not bear to think of such a friendly animal going into the cooking pot, he gave the woman who brought her five francs and set about making a pen, for hogs like to eat hens and, since hen's eggs are very valuable, no hog could be allowed to run wild through the grounds. After some time, however, Josephine disappeared and Schweitzer thought he had seen the last of her, but one day a native hunter brought her in again—

and received his gift—and once more Josephine was saved from the pot!

One of the missionaries decided to make the hog the subject of a sermon. He explained that when Josephine was wild she had belonged to no one, but now that she was tame, she belonged to someone and to take her was to steal. At that moment Josephine walked into the school-house and stood beside the preacher and then walked up and down the room, rubbing her dirty sides on everyone within reach until she got to Dr. Schweitzer, who gave her a swift kick. After that, every time the church bell rang, Josephine broke out of her pen and went to church. Then one day a hen was missing and its native owner blamed Josephine, so Dr. Schweitzer gave him a present. A little later the hog was caught killing a hen, and since that was something which could not possibly be allowed, Josephine shortly became ham and bacon.

Not long afterward, an officer stopped at the hospital and stayed for dinner. Bacon was served. "This is a rare treat," he said, and Dr. Schweitzer told him it was a tame hog which had been caught killing hens. "Oh," said the officer, "I once had a tame hog which I had raised from a bottle, but it was stolen. I called it Josephine."

"Then, my dear sir," said the doctor, "you are now eating Josephine."

A few months later Mrs. Schweitzer left to return to Europe. A short while in the tropics was apparently all that her health could stand, and it was a sad day for her husband when he had to see her depart.

Money continued to come in from European friends, so that the hospital was able to serve more natives and to supply them with basic foods, in addition to the expensive drugs they required for treatment. The hospital was well organized and firmly established.

Every Saturday all the women who have arrived with their sick relatives are called together by a nurse and directed to clear the grounds. First the wards are cleaned, then the streets and finally the grounds. The natives throw all cans into the long grass, just to get rid of them, and if they were allowed to remain, they would collect water and serve as breeding places for the malaria mosquito. During the clean-up procedure, the nurse walks continually around the group, for otherwise the workers keep on disappearing into the brush or into a ward and would soon leave the nurse alone on the job.

Many patients arrive for operations from the interior forests, first working their way to the river and then continuing by boat, when they manage to find one that will take them to the hospital. By the time they actually arrive, they are often weak from starvation. When they are cured and ready to return up-river, the hospital staff tries to beg a passage for them from any boat which stops at the hospital landing. Once the owner has agreed to take a passenger, it becomes the job of some doctor or nurse to keep the boat owner from realizing how time is passing while the others search the hospital for the patient, examine him to see if he is ready to travel and help him pack his belongings. These include rice in bottles, which

166

he has kept aside from the daily ration, bottles also being valuable as "money" in the interior. Then he is given a bag of salt so that he can buy what he needs along the way, either canoe passage or food. And at last he is escorted to the boat, for otherwise he would disappear to say good-bye to some friends and the boat would leave without him. When it is all over and the boat and the patient have safely departed, the hospital staff return to their duties completely exhausted.

In October 1931, Albert Schweitzer was invited to return to Frankfurt, in Germany, to give an address at the one hundredth anniversary of the death of the great German poet and dramatist, Goethe. Dr. Schweitzer accepted, for he had a full set of Goethe's works with him in Africa and so was able to complete his forthcoming lecture before his ship docked in Bordeaux, early in 1932, after an eighteen-days journey altogether. In March of that year, he stood up to give his oration in the opera house in Goethe's birthplace at the exact hour of the poet's death, one hundred years before. He spoke on the tragic times that were facing the peoples of the world, although he ended on a more optimistic note.

When the Frankfurt address was over, he started on a tour of lectures and organ recitals which took him again to Holland, Britain, Sweden, Germany and Switzerland. He arrived at one town in Holland a week before his recital was scheduled and spent his time cleaning the church organ. When the people heard it again, they could hardly believe it was the same instrument, the notes were so clear. Schweitzer's interest in organs was as keen as ever and this was not the first time he had overhauled a church organ before he played it.

As he traveled around, he collected many honors—honorary doctor degrees in divinity, music and law—for everywhere he went he was now acclaimed for his music or his literary work, as well as for his humanitarian work in Africa. His hours were long and his working day often lasted through the night, for wherever he went, he carried two large linen bags, one filled with letters that should be answered and the other to hold the letters as they were answered.

This was the pattern his life was now to take—several years in Africa alternating with two or three in Europe. (In 1933, his family had settled in Lausanne in Switzerland, where the climate suited Mrs. Schweitzer and there were good schools for Rhena.) Always in Europe his days were a mixture of lectures and recitals to raise money for his family and his hospital, with as much quiet for writing as he could squeeze into his busy life. While in Africa, he tried out many experiments, some of which worked and some did not, for the natives could never be relied upon to give any help in carrying them through.

At Lambaréné, Dr. Schweitzer had imported goats so that the Negro babies could have milk. It was impossible to keep these animals confined and they had to be allowed to run wild. But goats eat almost anything and the leaves and bark of the young fruit trees the doctor was trying to get started suffered the most. When, at last, posts and wire netting were put around each tree in order to protect it, the natives were too lazy to get firewood and pulled up the stakes for their cooking fires.

Joseph, who now was very proud of being the "doctor's first assistant" did not know how to save until Dr. Schweitzer made a money box into which he could put the money he was saving to buy a wife. He earned extra money by sitting up at night with very sick patients and by tips from the white patients. Joseph, however, was inclined to spend his wages as soon as he received them. One day, when he was with the doctor at the store, his eyes fell upon a pair of cracked and worthless patent leather shoes. They cost about a month's wages but he wanted them. The doctor, not wishing to have trouble with the store, tried to keep him from buying by giving him warning looks, then by nudging him in the side, and finally with a punch so painful that his "assistant" left the store. On the way home to the hospital, Dr. Schweitzer tried to explain how foolish such a purchase would be. Joseph listened in silence and the very next day returned to the store and bought the shoes. Was he not the doctor's first assistant? A man in such a position should wear shoes and, apart from his saving to buy a wife, all that he earned was spent on his personal appearance.

By 1937 Dr. Schweitzer realized that another war was inevitable and, because the First World War was still so vivid to the Schweitzers, they decided to get in touch with their friends in the United States, so that, in case Africa was cut off once again from European sources of supply, they could still get materials from America. In 1937 and again in 1938, while the doctor remained in Africa, Mrs. Schweitzer and Rhena went to America to lecture and raise funds for the hospital. As a result, the Albert Schweitzer Fellowship of America came into being, a society or community of those individuals who had suffered pain and wished to help others in their suffering.

In February of 1939, Albert Schweitzer arrived in France for a much needed rest, only to realize that war was very near and that he dared not risk being cut off from the hospital and the people to whom he had already given thirty years of his life; so he caught the return trip of the boat which had recently carried him to Europe from Africa.

As soon as he was back in Africa, he began to order supplies of medicine, equipment and food, for he knew that, once war broke out, they would never reach him. In May, both Mrs. Schweitzer and Rhena arrived at Lambaréné. For Rhena this was the first occasion, although she had longed to see her father's hospital. Now she was already married—to an organ builder. As a child she had heard much concerning the pets that came from the tropical forest and now she became acquainted with the monkeys, the five tame antelopes and the six baby chimpanzees which were the hospital pets just then. She was delighted with everything she saw. Her father was happy to have his family with him and to be able to share his African life with his daughter. Yet the visit was all too short and Rhena and Mrs. Schweitzer returned to Europe.

By September, Dr. Schweitzer decided to send back to their various villages everyone who was able to travel and in the future to take in only the most urgent cases. The patients begged to stay but the doctor was aware that food and medicine would soon run out, if he did not cut down right away. Also, if war came, his doctors and nurses would probably have to leave for service with the armies of France. Most of the supplies he had ordered earlier in the year arrived safely, in spite of the actual outbreak of war, but the last big shipment was lost when the boat which was carrying it was torpedoed and sunk in March 1940.

In the summer of 1941, Mrs. Schweitzer succeeded, after much difficulty, in getting from France to Lisbon, on the coast of Portugal, and then onto a steamer which landed her at a Portuguese African Colony, from where she managed to make her way to Lambaréné.

As the white assistants departed for Europe, Mrs. Schweitzer took over their work, serving as nurse, taking care of the operating equipment, keeping order generally and helping her husband with his correspondence.

With colonial France torn between the forces of General de Gaulle and those of the Vichy Government, the Lambaréné area was fought over, but both sides gave orders that the hospital was not to be bombed. In order, however, to keep stray shots from hitting the buildings, which was less than two miles from the fighting, Dr. Schweitzer had corrugated iron sheets put up as a fence on the Lambaréné side of the hospital. The Schweitzers

171

were not interned for, as natives of Alsace, they were now officially French citizens.

Rice became scarce and the mission schools had to close for lack of food. Yet the doors remained open to both whites and natives and was usually full. The government had started a camp farther up the river for sleeping sickness patients. The hospital continued to receive grim reminders that it was still on the edge of the jungle, for wild animals injured the natives, while elephants were forever destroying the banana plantation.

Just when supplies seemed about to give out, a shipment arrived which had been sent from America by the Albert Schweitzer Fellowship. It included such important items as large rubber gloves and bright new cooking pans, not to mention medicine and shoes. With this assistance and the continuing help of friends of the hospital in America, more patients could be taken care of.

The tropical climate and conditions were hard on those white people who could not return to Europe and the hospital became increasingly full with patients who were ill from a lack of calcium and other deficiencies of the tropics. Most of the medical and surgical work now fell to Dr. Schweitzer, who grew exceedingly tired.

At long last, on May seventh of 1945, as Dr. Schweitzer sat at his desk writing important letters to be picked up shortly by the river boat when it returned from upstream, a white patient who possessed a radio came in to tell him that the war was over. The doctor had to finish his letters or they would not be ready for the boat, so it was

172

well into the afternoon before he rang the hospital bell and told the joyful news to all who gathered around.

He had never felt so tired as he did at that moment, and still he had to drag himself to the plantation to see how the work there was progressing, for he had taken advantage of the lull in the timber trade to get native workers to clear more ground for growing more food. Night came before he was able to think what the ending of the war could mean in terms of help and equipment and much needed rest—and a sight of his three grandchildren whom he had never seen.

He reached for a book written in the sixth century B.C., by a Chinese philosopher, Laotse, and turned to what he had said about war.—"The slaughter of human beings in numbers should be lamented with tears of compassion, and whoever has conquered in battle should bear himself as if he were at a festival of mourning." With that Schweitzer turned to his piano and the nurses and patients heard a great recital, for their master played from his heart, which was full of both joy and pain.

Relief, however, was slow in coming, for it took months before the formalities could be met by those who were anxious to go to Lambaréné to assist the doctor. Moreover, the four years in the tropics had been particularly hard on Mrs. Schweitzer and she felt compelled to return to Europe before the 1945 wet season set in. Her visits to Africa since that time have been short and during the dry season only. The doctor, however, is better made to

173

stand the climate and since the end of the war his life goes on much as it did before.

Each evening when the Catholic Mission bells ring out for prayers, a pelican leaves his fishing ground on the exposed bank of the river and flies to his roost on a trellis above the steps leading to the veranda of Dr. Schweitzer's house. Here he spends the black tropical night standing guard. This he does well for he will only allow the doctor and his staff to pass. All others receive hard pecks and many are the presents the doctor has had to give to soothe an angry native who came too close to the pelican. The pelican has been there for many years. It was one of three babies brought by a native who had killed its mother on the sand banks and then brought the youngsters to the hospital in order to get the usual reward for saving life! At the time, they were too small either to fish or to fly, and small fish had to be caught for them and placed within their beaks. Eventually, they grew their flight feathers and learned to fly but one was always smaller and slower than the others. It became known to everyone as "Monsieur le Pelican."

With the coming of the dry season, the usual flock of pelicans from inland waters arrived and the three hospital pets flew up, circled with the newcomers and flew with the wild birds to the sand banks. Everyone thought that this was the last they would see of them, but when the rains came and the birds returned inland, Monsieur le Pelican remained behind. He was fed fish from the kitchen until the next dry season came, when he again joined the birds fishing on the banks, though every night he returned to stand guard at Dr. Schweitzer's door. On one occasion he had a leg broken, probably by a native who caught him stealing fish. Each day, someone carried him to the sand banks so that he could fish as usual, and at the end of the day he was carried back to his hospital perch.

Albert Schweitzer was seventy years old when the war ended, and from all over Europe and America his Fellowships sent greetings to him and money for the hospital. The money was greatly needed, for prices were rising and the cost of maintaining the hospital service for the Africans was greater than ever before. More money was necessary and so was additional manpower. Dr. Schweitzer performed the work of a thirty-year-old man and each day he inspected all parts of the settlement. He had to do this, in spite of the fatigue which he felt continually. He had aged greatly in body, but in mind he was as alert as ever and his fingers and his feet were still well able to play Bach, in fact even better than before. Every night he played music and wrote, long after the rest of the hospital was asleep.

He stayed on at the hospital for several years after the fighting had ended—until it was once again supplied with doctors and nurses. Not until 1948 did the very weary man return to the quiet and refreshing mountain air of the Black Forest, to regain the strength necessary to continue his work. A large part of this visit to Europe was spent in becoming acquainted with his four grandchildren. He had always loved children and it is easy to picture the hours he spent telling his grandchildren the stories of the antelopes and monkeys and hippos; and to see the youngest sitting on his lap as he helped her pick out her first musical notes on the piano.

For a good many years, Dr. Schweitzer had received invitations to visit America, but there had never seemed to be time for it. However, in July of 1949, he made the trip, in order to give the memorial address on Goethe before the Goethe Foundation, at Aspen, Colorado, in celebration of the two hundredth anniversary of the poet's birth.

He enjoyed his visit to North America and in crossing the great plains by train was especially interested in the large herds of cattle and sheep grazing in the fields. A friend told him that only the winter before it had been necessary to drop food to these animals from airplanes, because of the deep snow drifts. He was much impressed with this concern for life and thought that nowhere had he encountered more feeling for living creatures than in the United States.

Before Dr. Schweitzer returned to Europe, the University of Chicago gave him an honorary doctor's degree and he was able to enjoy visits to both New York and Boston. Yet time was pressing and soon he was in Africa again.

CHAPTER 14

Europe and Africa

At Home in Europe

FOR the past few years Albert Schweitzer has divided his time, as usual, between Africa and Europe. In Europe, his home is still Günsbach, the little town in the Munster valley where his roots have grown so deep. The village has changed but little since he lived there as a boy. The houses cluster about the church on the side of the hill, while the four hundred inhabitants work in a cotton factory in Munster and grow grapes at home. All are his friends and he feels he is a part of them and of their lives.

Dr. and Mrs. Schweitzer still live in "the house that Goethe built," on the outskirts of the village, where they can see across the open fields and vineyards. So does his secretary, Mrs. Martin, who serves as his permanent staff, carrying on the work of ordering supplies, receiving money and answering letters while the doctor is in Africa. To Günsbach come the gifts collected by such organizations as "The Friends of Lambaréné" and the "Albert Schweitzer Fellowship"—gifts which make it possible to continue the service to the African natives.

When at home at Günsbach, Dr. Schweitzer lives a very simple life. He rises at seven and, after breakfast, goes to his room to write, a room which is much like a monk's cell and one which opens above the street so that he can see his neighbors in their gardens or as they pass along. Every so often he looks up from his writing to wave to a friend dressed in the light blue overall and apron which is the uniform of the vineyard workers. And he is never too busy to talk about his neighbor's crops and harvest.

In the late morning, he leaves his desk and walks to the village to visit a friend or meet a train or keep an appointment, returning in time for lunch. The dining table, which seats twelve, is usually filled with his friends or often with strangers who have come to call. He never did understand the mysteries of housekeeping and expects his womenfolk to arrange for extra places, just as he had done in Lambaréné. When the hospital is full, he tells a nurse to make arrangements and no one is turned away. So it is in Günsbach. There is always room for those who come.

Mrs. Martin, as his secretary, tries to protect him from the curious or from those visitors who would stay too long, keeping him from his work, but he so loves meeting people that her job is not an easy one.

After lunch he writes again or sees visitors, and when the afternoon shadows begin to lengthen he goes for walks

178

over the hills and fields, or up to the church to play the organ.

People often wait in the street outside his house to see if he is going to go to the church, and when he does start up the steep hill they follow, hoping to hear a recital. They take their seats silently as their musician friend sits down at the first organ he ever played, when he was only eight years old and his feet could barely touch the pedals. He had the fine old organ rebuilt in 1928 and now we are able to hear recordings he has made and enjoy for ourselves its wonderful tone. He may play a group of Bach's chorals and, after changing the stops, perhaps a fugue. No one moves in the church until the last note dies away, and he stands up and closes and locks the organ. The recital is over and the people follow their doctor out into the quiet twilight. Then he turns to shake hands with those he has not seen for a while and to ask about their families and their grapes, or to greet strangers who have found their way to the doctor's town and will never forget these moments in the Günsbach church. Then they all move off to their own homes and their waiting suppers. Sight-seers may find it difficult to discover him, but sincere visitors will find his hand outstretched at any time.

After the evening meal, Dr. Schweitzer and his secretary work together on the letters which arrive by the hundreds. The room they work in is filled with reminders of Lambaréné; pictures of the hospital and the natives hang on the walls and on his desk stand many gifts from grateful

179

patients—mostly crudely carved animals in ebony or ivory. Often the doctor works on alone until his is the only light in the village still burning. Yet no matter how late it is or how tired he may be, he sits at his piano to play for a while. At last, however, he turns out the light and the little village of Günsbach is finally dark.

At Home in Africa

For long periods at a time the doctor's home is at the edge of the jungle. He has always been wise enough to recognize the fact that his Lambaréné hospital, situated as it is almost within the forest, can never be like the hospitals of Europe and America, where white walls and sterile conditions are felt to be so important. He has never wasted time attempting the impossible and has simply given his love and service as freely as he could. The Lambaréné hospital is like no other and cannot be compared with other institutions.

Yet the hospital as it is today is very different from what it was at first. Now Dr. Schweitzer walks among the forty-five buildings on the hills which slope to the river's edge, shaded by palms and mango trees. No garden flowers grow along the edge of the paths, for he will not have flowers cut for use as table decorations, since for him flowers are alive and he reveres all life. Wild flowers would in any case have little chance to grow in the hospital grounds, for the animals are everywhere, most of them having been raised from helpless young.

There is always much activity but no one seems to be in a hurry, not even the doctor as he walks through the grounds, inspecting every corner, for he is followed by his dogs Tchu-Fchu and Gropette. When he meets Julot, a chimpanzee, on the path, he stops to pet him, and whenever he rests for a moment on a stump of a tree, there is sure to be a pet antelope close enough to lick his arm for the sake of the salty taste.

The hospital has changed in many ways and one of the most important is that there are now fifteen acres of vegetable garden during each dry season. The natives water and weed it under the supervision of one of the white members of the hospital staff. The orchard, too, furnishes a great quantity of fruit, for now each tree is carefully fertilized by goat and antelope manure to replace the topsoil washed away by the heavy rains. Oranges, mandarins, grapefruit, guava, avocados, and mangos furnish the table with a wide variety, while palm trees supply all the oil that is needed for cooking.

New equipment is constantly being added to the hospital and at last, after all these years, there is a gasoline-driven electricity generator which makes it possible for the first time to use an X-ray machine. Dr. Schweitzer no longer carries the load alone for now there are many doctors and nurses to help him, all working for a bare living wage and out of love for their fellow men. Albert Schweitzer is their inspiration.

French is the language officially spoken at the hospital, but the five hundred native patients now treated each month speak ten different dialects. In addition to these regular patients there are the many lepers and the numerous white patients. Almost every known tropical disease is met with and treated.

Yet some things remain unchanged. The sick still arrive in dugout canoes, accompanied by their families and all their possessions—clothes tied in dirty rag bundles, cooking pans, bananas, and all their fears and superstitions. To leave any belongings behind in their villages would be to lose them forever.

Understanding all of this is necessary for effecting cures. Dr. Schweitzer knows too well that only by making his patients feel at home can he hope to cure them, for if they are frightened, they will not stay nor will they come again. If a patient should become homesick for his family, he would leave whether he was well enough to do so or not, and when he is well enough to travel, his family are needed to take him home again by dugout canoe many hundred miles up the river. Families are needed for cooking the patient's food. The food is issued by the hospital but each family cooks its own on an open fire. Relatives are also needed to help nurse the patient and to see that an enemy tribesman in the next bed does not poison his neighbor. And besides all this, Dr. Schweitzer believes that the natives should pay with some service for the care that the hospital gives, particularly since the hospital itself is maintained by gifts.

A new river steamer now docks at the landing, covering the distance up the river in twenty-four hours instead of the forty-eight required by the old *Alembe* which first brought the Schweitzers to Lambaréné. Yet when the whistle blows, everyone who can walk goes down to the river to help unload the boxes marked A.S.B. (the B stands for Bresslau, Mrs. Schweitzer's maiden name). The three letters are recognised all along the coast and up the rivers, and if any box goes astray, it is soon restored, for everyone knows that A.S.B. means "the Doctor."

It has never been easy and the last few years have been particularly hard for Dr. Schweitzer. No matter how hard he tries, he cannot do half of the things he would like to. He is tired, terribly tired.

Yet in 1943, when a new drug for treatment of leprosy was developed in America, he applied it with remarkable results. The native telegraph system, the tom-tom, spread the word from village to village throughout the forest, and the lepers who had been cast out of their villages to wander alone in the jungle heard the news and made their way to the Lambaréné hospital. It meant more expense and work for the hospital but the doctor could not deprive the unfortunate beings of their chance for a new life. As usual, he faced the problem realistically and started to build a leper hospital about one quarter mile from the settlement. How he would find the extra money needed to maintain and expand it he did not know, but the way came when in 1952 he was awarded the Nobel Peace Prize of thirty-three thousand dollars.

For a man of seventy-eight to start to build a new hospital under the particular existing circumstances was a tremendous undertaking. The top of a hill had to be leveled off or built up in various places. The natives could not understand the need for this and would not do it unless Dr. Schweitzer himself stayed on the site during all of the working hours. He drafted all the leper patients who were able to assist at all, which came to about sixty, and each worked according to his ability and state of health. Baskets were filled with dirt and carried on poles by two men, while the women, of whom there were twelve, carried smaller baskets. Finally, a friendly timber merchant came to the rescue and loaned five hundred and fifty feet of rails and three rail trucks. On these the dirt was more easily taken from the hill top to the places where it was needed. Now, instead of heavy work, the natives had a plaything and, if not constantly watched, after filling the cars, they would let them race to the bottom of the incline out of control, causing accidents. The doctor's work was increased for he had to be with them every moment.

Dr. Schweitzer has always held to the principle that those who find care and shelter in his hospital which is financed by the gifts of other people should repay with labor whenever possible. The workers, however, receive some money each week. They are also given their clothes, and two or three times a week some extra sweets and sugar. Besides this, they receive training in building and they learn carpentry, which they can practice in their villages after they return home. For this reason, Dr. Schweitzer only uses tools which are available to the natives of the jungle.

This eliminates any use of power tools and slows up the work, but it is in keeping with his attitude of service.

Every morning at eight, all the leper patients who are able report for roll call and from that moment they have to be watched or else they will return to their huts or go fishing. After being given their tools, they will drop them in the bushes on the way to the building site and disappear into the jungle. Once on the site, they are incapable of doing any work unless continually supervised, and if the doctor turns his back, they put down their tools until he returns to help them.

It required all of Dr. Schweitzer's past experience to build the leper hospital and no one else could do it. In time, however, they leveled a place six hundred and fifty by two hundred and sixty feet, and at the end of a year and a half there were many new buildings with cement block foundations, hardwood beams, corrugated iron roofs, and walls of raffia and slender bamboo poles. Now there is room for three hundred leper cases and every morning at the ringing of a bell the sick line up for treatment. The treatment consists of injection of Promin or a Deasone pill, together with vitamin pills and a glass of milk. You would be surprised to see the number of small children who stand in the leper line. After treatment, they run off happily to their school, where they learn French and write letters on a smooth board, using a leaf to erase them and clean the board.

The Nobel Prize money started the hospital and the money raised by the Norwegian people made it possible to finish it. Today, the lepers are filled with hope and, due to modern medical science and to Dr. Schweitzer and his friends, they face a new future.

The Birthday

On the morning of January 14, 1955, Albert Schweitzer wakened to the sound of the singing of an old Alsatian carol, for in Lambaréné it is the custom that someone who is celebrating a birthday should be treated to an early serenade by the nurses and doctors.

At breakfast, there were gifts at Dr. Schweitzer's place at the table. His wife was there to sit by his side, for she had flown to Lambaréné to be with her husband on his eigthieth birthday. Someone put on a record of the church bells in his homeland in the Munster valley. As he listened, his thoughts went to those cold, crisp birthdays of his youth. He would like this day to pass as any other day, for he is too conscious of the passage of time and how little is left in which to accomplish all that he wished to do.

Messages and letters had been coming in for days from all parts of the world, from friends wishing him health and time to accomplish what he yet wanted to do. In many distant places, special celebrations were planned, with special music played in his honor and orations delivered on the life and work of a man who had given up a brilliant career in theology, philosophy and music to become a medical man in darkest Africa. They honored

186

this man of mercy in their own ways, but Albert Schweitzer had still to go about his work as he had always done. He felt very tired and still lame from an accident he suffered while making his last voyage to Africa.

As he left the dining hall he found his friends, the natives, waiting to offer their gifts to their beloved doctor. They presented their most valued possessions—a few eggs, a chicken, fruit, and crude carvings in ivory or ebony. His eyes twinkled with pleasure as he thanked each one in turn. By request, no newspaper men were present to report on the celebration, for he wanted no fanfare, only to be allowed to go on with his work. All morning he spent with the sick or the dying and with the workmen in the leper village, where the patients were busy building terraces in front of the hospital buildings. Throughout the day, more patients arrived in their long dugouts, while others, now well enough to go home, departed with waves of farewell from the doctors and nurses.

American friends arrived for a visit and Albert Schweitzer switched easily from French to English. When lunch time arrived, thirty-six people sat at the long table, down the center of which green leaves and bananas, lemons, apples and breadfruit were placed for decoration. Mrs. Schweitzer sat on her husband's right and everyone knew he was in a festive mood, for he laughed and talked more than usual. Before the meal was underway, he rose to give a speech, which was a surprise to all. He wanted to welcome his visitors and to say he was glad to be at Lambaréné at this time, since he felt it to be so much his home. He spoke of his daughter, who also celebrated her birthday on this day. He stood tall and erect, laughing easily, and as he sat down it was obvious to everyone that he was enjoying his birthday.

After lunch, however, he disappeared into his room, in order to write. Later, he was carried in a litter, because of his knee injury, to the burying grounds, to say a prayer at the funeral service of a native worker. The work of the hospital went on as usual and the doctor's day was full.

When evening came and the sky glowed with the sunset colors and the air was blue with the smoke of hundreds of small cooking fires, Dr. Schweitzer made his nightly round of the sick, saying "good night, my children," and hearing their answering "good night." Satisfied that all was well, he joined his fellow workers at their evening meal and once again was jovial and eager for conversation. After a while, he conducted a vesper service and played the piano while the whole group sang a hymn. When he departed for his room, his dog followed closely at his heels. He stopped to pet Erica and Jagagruno, two baby antelopes recently raised on a bottle. He sat at his desk, made from the packing boxes which held the first medicines he brought with him to Africa, more than forty years ago. Sizi, a kitten who received her first milk from a medicine dropper held by the doctor, jumped onto the desk, demanding attention. He stroked her back with one hand while he wrote with the other.

There were many letters containing birthday greetings yet to be read. Each envelope was carefully opened and a hole punched in one corner. Several of these were tied together with a piece of string, for nothing has ever been wasted at Lambaréné and the habit is strong. Most of Schweitzer's seventeen published books were first written on just such papers. When he finished writing, he hung the papers on a nail in the wall, just out of reach of curious antelopes. He remembered too well having to rewrite a part of the first book on civilization because it had been eaten by a hungry young antelope. And he knew now that he has no more time for rewriting, for his flame of life is burning low. His mind was as alert as ever but his fatigue increased with every passing day.

Albert Schweitzer moved quietly to his piano and his still flexible fingers played the opening chords of the *Toccata and Fugue in D Minor,* in a triumphant and magnificent interpretation of Bach, played by a master who fully understands his music.

This music was heard throughout the hospital and the nurses and doctors, tired after their strenuous day's work in the heat of the tropics, listened and relaxed and went to sleep. The natives forgot their pain—and Albert Schweitzer found rest himself. In the morning a new day and another year would begin in the life of the man of mercy.

CHAPTER 15

The Meaning of
Albert Schweitzer

WHY has Albert Schweitzer become such a towering figure in the world today? Why do people everywhere, young and old, pay him honor, whether or not they have read his writings or known of him for long? What makes him seem so important?

He has written many books, but there have been many better writers. He is a good philosopher but not the greatest. He is a first rate musician and an authority on Bach and organ music, but that is not the reason. His hospital in Africa is well suited to the needs of jungle people but there are bigger and better hospitals in other parts of tropical Africa. All of these are part of the answer but only part. For what people recognize in Albert Schweitzer is not his talents as a thinker or musician or even as a physician but the fact that, above all else, he is a man—a human being of the kind that everyone should be to the best of his or her ability. Like Jesus, whom he admires so much, Albert Schweitzer has felt love and concern for all mankind and has had the courage to put his feelings into action and to live his life accordingly. Even when a boy, he was able to see himself as an individual amidst all of his fellow beings, to realize that life is a mixture of joy and suffering but that some get mostly joy and more get mostly suffering. He saw himself as part of the brotherhood of man but as an individual with more talent and greater strength than most, and he saw clearly in that bright early morning at Günsbach what he ought to do. Many people have known as much about themselves and their obligations on this earth, but only a few of them have had the moral strength and force of character to put all else aside and live according to their convictions. Albert Schweitzer has been one of these and in this twentieth century of ours his example stands out like a beacon. We recognize his love for all of us, for every human being and for everything that lives, and this heartfelt, all-embracing love shows in his face, in his kindly eyes, and in everything he does. We recognize this love and respond to it, but even this does not fully explain what is so striking about Albert Schweitzer and why we are so impressed.

Hidden away for forty years in the African jungle, he has become a force for peace, civilization and culture, primarily because of his personality. He is essentially simple and dislikes the fuss which is being made over him. He belongs to no particular church and has no formal religion, but his feeling of reverence for life and his belief that we are surrounded by more mystery than we can comprehend indicates a deeply religious nature. This combination of reverence and awe, together with his intense awareness of human brotherhood, partly explains him. By itself, however, this would not mean very much. He has made it into a powerful force, a will to act, so that he has put into practical form all that he feels and believes. He has acted according to his convictions, with a courage and determination which is all too rare. Albert Schweitzer gave up a way of life to which he was dearly attached in order to do what he felt he ought to do, and the fact that he did so has given people faith that they themselves have the same capacity to do what they feel is right.

Yet more than this, Albert Schweitzer, with his powerful and active mind, has faced our human situation frankly, which is that we are all involved in a universe whose mystery is overwhelming and that suffering is the rule and not the exception for most living things. There are but two choices. One is to give up and say there is nothing we can do about it and the other is to take a stand with all the powers and strength that we have, and, with all of our spirit and personality, to do everything we can to make life what we think it should be.

By never giving in, by asserting his own faith in goodness, by acknowledging both the mystery and the force of love, Albert Schweitzer has shown that man can be magnificently courageous and that the truly religious man is one who will fight until death for the preservation and well-being of all life. More than anything else, it is this figure of a man, standing alone and unafraid, willing to stake all that he possesses, all that he is, and all of his existence in a strong challenge against disease, misery and cruelty, that demands our admiration. While he never says so and may not even know it—all his actions speak for him. They say, "Here is a man, as a man should be. Go thou and be likewise." People know this and accept it, everywhere. And because of Albert Schweitzer, many people will, in their own particular individual ways, live better and more constructive lives, inspired by knowing what one man can do.

Jacquelyn Berrill

was born in Kentucky, graduated from the University of Toledo, and took post-graduate work at New York University. She did group work with teen-age girls in the Jackson and Lansing, Michigan, Y.W.C.A., before her marriage to Dr. N. J. Berrill, a Professor of Zoology at McGill University, Montreal.

Jacquelyn Berrill writes and illustrates her books, surrounded by and taking part in the busy activities of her three children—Peggy, just starting to teach, and teen-agers Elsilyn and Michael. Her hobbies include photography, block-printing, rug making, interior decorating and gardening.

The family spend their winters in the center of Montreal and long holidays at their cottage in Boothbay Harbor, Maine, where they have a one-room cottage which they finished themselves, and where the children have their own house on top of a large rock which the last glacier conveniently left in their back yard.

Index

197